THE OUTRAGEOUS
LIFE AND TIMES OF A
FOOTBALL GUY

TONY SIRAGUSA

with DON YAEGER

 CROWN ARCHETYPE · NEW YORK

Library of Congress Cataloging-in-Publication Data is available upon request.

ISBN 978-0-307-95598-2
eISBN 978-0-307-98564-4

Printed in the United States of America

Book design by Maria Elias
Jacket design by Nupoor Gordon
Jacket photographs by Scott McDermott

10   9   8   7   6   5   4   3   2   1

First Edition

To all the people who told me I couldn't do it.

CONTENTS

CONTENTS

01

DRAFT DAY

With apologies to Dickens, the third weekend in April 1990 was the best of times . . . and it was the worst of times. One of the most improbable stories in the NFL—my story—goes back to April 22–23, 1990, the weekend of the NFL draft that year: two days of hell for me and my family. My beautiful mother, Rosemarie, invited the whole world to our little house in Kenilworth, New Jersey, to watch the draft.

And watch. And watch. And watch.

All twelve rounds of it. Minute after minute, my mom, my brothers Pete and Elio, and my then-girlfriend and now-wife Kathy (she's been with me since high school) were watching as player after player got picked. Twelve rounds and 331 players, including seven of my teammates from the University of Pittsburgh who were selected. But not me. These days, the NFL has only seven rounds for the draft, and it's a struggle to make the league if you're undrafted. These days you might have two guys on the fifty-three-man roster each year who were undrafted. So think about it: back when I was coming out of Pitt, the league was taking like five rounds of guys who today would have a hard time getting drafted—and I still didn't get taken.

This was like being the last kid picked on the playground. You know when you divide up teams and that last guy is there and the best guy says, "Whatever, we'll take him"? That's what my NFL draft weekend was like for me. I had been here before. Growing up, I was good in football, wrestling, and baseball. I was a good all-around athlete. Good, but not great. I wasn't like The Natural when I was seven years old, like some of these guys. I was always bigger and stronger than most kids, so people thought I was older than I actually was. People would say, "Oh, you must be twelve." I'm like, "No, I'm nine." I also used to hang out with older kids because of my older brother Pete. And I also acted older. I didn't back down from anybody, even when I got my ass kicked. I'd tell off the older kids, maybe flip them off. They'd chase me down, they'd beat me up, and then I'd tell them off again. I was a real smart-ass.

Anyway, when I was twelve, I was playing Little League baseball and they picked the all-star team. It came down to the last cut, and I didn't make it. I was the first alternate or whatever they call it. So I walked home the whole way from the field along the railroad tracks that went by my house, crying my eyes out. I'm pissed, I'm embarrassed, I'm hurt, the whole thing. It was like that spark that we all get in our gut when we think nobody wants us. This burning desire goes off in you. At least it did with me. This was the first kind of defining moment for me. I got home, and we had a little pool in the back, so I washed my face off and then went inside. I never told my mom what happened. Then the coaches called up a few days later and told me, "Oh, this kid got hurt, you're in, we need you." I thought to myself, *These SOBs didn't pick me, okay, I'll show them.* I knew the other kids weren't as good as me, so I had to go prove it.

Now, part of my problem up to then was that I was always thinking too much, being too careful. I was actually terrified to swing the bat. I don't really know why. I wasn't scared of the ball. I think I was just scared that I wouldn't be perfect. I didn't want to disappoint anyone; I thought, *Let me just get a walk and I'll be fine.* My mother used to yell from the stands all the time, "Swing the bat!" Well, it turns out that's probably why I didn't get picked in the first place, and now I had to show these guys I was actually good enough, that I was actually better than everybody else. So in the second game we played, we had the bases loaded with two outs in the bottom of the last inning. The kid who was supposed to bat was having a horrible time. He had some problem, and he was like crying or something, and his mother was coming around going, "Honey, is something wrong? Are you okay, sweetie?" The problem was, he was kind of a mama's boy, a pussy. Anyway, the coach looked at me and said, "Goose, you're up next." I was like, *Holy crap, this is great.* I get the helmet, I'm looking for my bat—I'm all jacked up. Before, I was a little scared to swing for whatever reason. Now, as I go up to the plate, I'm deciding I'll swing as hard as I can at the first pitch: I'm going to kill this ball. I get up there, the pitcher winds up, and I just remember how slow he seemed to bring the ball. He threw, and I think I probably closed my eyes and swung.

It's like this awesome dream. There was this two-story building just past the right-field fence. It's still there if you drive through town. When we were kids, that building was mythic. My brother's friends used to talk about how nobody could ever hit the ball over that building. It was kind of like in that movie *The Sandlot*—how they talk about what it's like to hit the ball into the junkyard in center field. Anyway, as the ball was coming, the moment was like something from a movie for me. Really, if the pitcher had thrown the ball over the backstop, I would have swung anyway, that's how determined I was. I swung as hard as I could, and *bam!* I hit the ball. The ball cleared the building for a grand slam: the ultimate scenario. I remember coming around the bases and everybody was jacked up and excited. All the way around, I'm thinking, *These assholes didn't want to pick me.* I can remember all the players and the coaches standing there at home plate as I turned third base and headed home. And that's when I knew I could do this. It's funny to think sometimes, what would have happened if I struck out? Would that one moment have completely changed me? Right then and there, that became the theme for my life. *I know I can do this.*

Ten years later, it's all happening again as I wait for a chance to play in the NFL. To add a nice kick in the teeth, add the misery of practically every person in my family and every person in town stopping by at one time or another to look in on what's going on. After a while, people don't even ask, "Did he get drafted yet?" They come in, give that little pathetic smile like they don't know what to say, and kind of move on. My mother is making macaroni the whole weekend and putting on a brave face, saying, "Don't worry about him, he's going to be okay."

I even get a call from Jimmy Johnson in the middle of the whole thing. Jimmy, who I work with at FOX now, was coaching at Dallas, but I knew him from way before that. Jimmy was coaching at the University of Miami when I was in high school, and he recruited me. That's a whole 'nother story I'll get into later. Anyway, he calls me and says, "Hey, what's going on?"—like I somehow have some answer for why I'm not getting drafted. I answer, "Nothing, what's going on with you?" What am I supposed to say?

Here's the funny part of that call. The reason Jimmy has called me is that he thinks I called him. As the draft is going on, some of my friends, including this guy Crazy Mike Carisino, start calling the Dallas Cowboys. The only thing is, they call claiming to be me and leave messages saying, "Jimmy, this is Tony Siragusa, you need to draft me!" Crazy Mike comes over, and I tell him that Johnson called. He tells me what he and the guys did. I'm like, what are you doing to me? He says back to me, "You should have told him to draft you."

All the while, my older brother Pete and my younger brother Elio are getting more and more pissed off, but they're not saying a thing. Kathy is there too, but she's not letting it bother her. She's just there to support me, comfort me. Talk about somebody who's devoted. I know plenty of women from being in the league who wouldn't have stuck around for that. She reminds me of that a lot. She says, "I was with you when you had nothing."

Me, of course I'm pissed too, but I'm taking it all in, internalizing the whole thing. It's like I'm just in a fog. Just the year before, I had lost my dad to a heart attack. And that was after spending a whole year away from football because of a knee injury. Then I went back to college and got jerked around by my coaches. Now, after all of that crap, one pick after another goes by, one round after another goes by, and I'm thinking, *They took that freaking guy, are you kidding me?* I get so fed up, I go to play golf at one point. Me, Kathy, and my brothers go to Weequahic Park Golf Course in Newark, New Jersey, and hit the ball around. I think I shot the best round of my life, like a 77 or something. I'm a wreck out there on the course, but I'm sinking putt after putt after putt. It was unreal.

Another time we go out in front of the house and play some basketball on the rim my dad put up on one of the trees way back in the day. We like to call the basketball court our "office," where we go to work out any problems. Siragusa family basketball isn't exactly artistic stuff, you have to understand. Me and my brothers were all really good high school wrestlers. I won a state title, Elio finished second, and Pete was actually probably the best of the three of us. Our game is no blood, no foul. We have a little tradition that we play when things are a little tense. This is a good day for that. We also played before all our weddings. Somebody usually ends up getting a bloody nose. It's a mess.

After the draft was over, Pete brought me out to the garage and wanted me to start working out with the weights right then and there. He cleared out the whole garage and starts saying, "You gotta get ready, you gotta get ready to kill somebody when you get out there." He was so angry because, for him, what I was doing was partly his dream too. My uncle Marty, my mom's brother, was like that too. Half the town was like that. They were so pissed off, it was almost like it happened to them. They felt like they were getting slapped in the face after all their hard work to support me along the way. I felt that from them, and it was a good thing. It was pure support, pure love from people who really care about you and want to see you succeed.

The thing is that, as the draft unraveled, I was not letting anybody see me lose control. I wasn't embarrassed, I was shocked. And then that spark started up again. I remember thinking at one point, *What am I going to do now, work construction?* I had a million scenarios playing out in my head. I used to work for another one of my uncles in construction, which I didn't want to do, and he made sure to discourage me as much as possible. He would make me carry cinder blocks all day long and do other kinds of crazy shit just to discourage me from wanting to do that crap. Trust me, he got the message across. One thing was for certain—I wasn't going to do that, at least not on those terms. If you want me to do something fun like build a man cave or open a restaurant, I'm all over it. But being a pack mule hauling cinder blocks? Oh, hell no.

Really, I felt more like I somehow let down everybody in my family and my neighborhood—all the people who helped me out. With me, family is the most important thing, and this hurt. The other part of me was also feeling that much stronger because I know this is the kind of support I have. I know who's really behind me. I've known that my whole life. I'm going to get into my hometown in the next chapter, but let me just say here, that's where my real strength comes from. Yeah, I'm six-foot-three, three-hundred-something pounds, and all that, but there's plenty of big guys in the NFL. The difference is not how big and strong you are, it's what's behind you. It's your foundation. My foundation is rock-solid: from my mom and late father, to my brothers, to everybody around me.

That's why, even on one of my worst days, I didn't lose sight of making it. This is when I'm at my best. I love it. I thrive on it. If you want to get me fired up, don't pick me. Let me be the last kid picked. Bet against me—it'll be the worst decision you ever made. It's like I need somebody to bet against me. If everybody bets on my side, it's a lot harder for me to concentrate. But when I'm the underdog, watch out. It's like when I play golf and I'm in a foursome where the other three guys are scratch golfers. I'll stay right with them, shot for shot. Then, when my team needs a big drive at the end, I'm the guy who will make it happen. Maybe all the other guys hit their shots in the woods, but I'll come through with the shot right in the middle of the fairway.

When I have that kind of pressure, watch out. When there's no way something can be done, I'll be there and get it done. I'll give you an example. Former NFL quarterback Ron Jaworski has a golf tournament every year down in Atlantic City, and it's a single elimination. There are ten former NFL guys who get paired up with ten celebrities. Everybody tees off, alternating shots, worst scores out. The winner gets $30,000. This one year, we go through and get to the last hole, and it's me and former

Washington quarterback Joe Theismann. The guy drives on a par four. I go and put one in front of the green. He flubs one and chips it on. I have a thirty-foot putt. Theismann has maybe a ten-foot putt. It's five hundred people around the thing. I just go over and I know I'm going to make the putt. It's not like I have to make it for my life to be great, but when the pressure's on and I have to make this for $30,000? Done. Other people, when they face this type of situation, they just fold. If there's a natural disaster, come to my house because I will survive. I'm just a survivor. I went up to the putt, looked at it, focused in, saw how the putt would roll in, went down, and putted. I sunk it.

To me, being a survivor comes from having support. Real support. A family, a village, a city . . . everybody behind you. When you have that kind of support, you don't wallow. I didn't get drafted? Fine, big deal. You know what? I've faced worse, including having a gun pointed in my mouth during a fight. By the time I got to draft day, I didn't have the anterior cruciate ligament (ACL) in my left knee, and the ACL in my right knee had been repaired. The ACL is like the linchpin of your knee. There are four ligaments, but the ACL is the one basically in the middle of the knee, holding the whole thing together and making sure the whole joint is stable. You lose that sucker, you're pretty much out for a year. The rehabilitation from an ACL takes like six months, minimum. And that's if you're repairing it. For me, I just had one of them taken out completely and went the hard way by reconditioning my whole body. I'll get into that later. Suffice to say, I'm a freaking medical miracle. Forget the NFL—I probably shouldn't have been drafted in a bocce ball league.

Both knees got messed up when I was at the University of Pittsburgh. If you have one ACL repair, that's a red flag to NFL teams. They automatically look at that and think, *Big-ass risk, we're going to take that guy late in the draft.* I trumped that because I didn't even have an ACL in one leg. I didn't just get red-flagged, I got black-flagged. The bad part is, I didn't really know that. Before the draft, I had people in my ear telling me I was going to maybe be a second- or third-round pick, maybe fourth. I was feeling pretty good about myself. Now this was before the draft became this big, made-for-TV BS event. You'd get some big coverage of the first round or so, but after that nobody really paid attention.

Now this shit is out of control. They have seven rounds, almost half of what they had before, and it takes three days. Hell, it takes one day just to get through the first round. You wonder why some of these rookies come in the league with egos like they actually have done something? This is why. We make these guys into freaking stars before they've been to one practice. It takes two months just to get them to realize they don't know diddly about how to play.

Back when I was coming out, nobody gave a damn about the draft except the players themselves and their families. These days it's a TV spectacle. It's like freaking Christmas in April for NFL fans. In April your team takes five or six new guys, and everybody thinks they should be buying Super Bowl tickets because every one of those guys is going to be a Pro Bowler, the way the media blows them up. Nowadays we got Mel Kiper Jr. and Mike Mayock telling us all this information about guys who get drafted in the fifth round, like all these guys have a chance to be stars. Fifth round? You know how many fifth-rounders I've seen come and go in my career? Shit, going in the first round doesn't mean anything. You want proof, just look at the year I came out. I went undrafted, and the number-one overall pick was Jeff George.

Yeah, Jeff George, my eventual teammate with the Indianapolis Colts. Yeah, Jeff George who was supposed to be the savior of the Colts, along with all those other stars we took way up high in the draft some year or another, like Steve Emtman and Quentin Coryatt, the number-one and number-two overall picks by the Colts in 1992. Those guys all got taken way ahead of me, but I always felt I was just as good as them. In my early days with the Colts, we were the champions of the NFL draft. You could put the crown on our head in April, but come September we were nowhere to be found. We would take all these big guys who looked like Tarzan but played like Jane.

I ended up in Indianapolis because there weren't a lot of options. After I went undrafted, I had to find a spot to play. My agent, Gus Sunseri, a good Italian guy from Pittsburgh, was getting calls after the draft. The first call I got was from Buddy Ryan, who was the head coach in Philadelphia at the time. Now, considering the success I had later in my career in Baltimore with Buddy's son Rex, you might be thinking, *Well, that's natural, go play for a Ryan.*

Forget about it. Do you know how stacked the Philadelphia defense was at that time? The Eagles were freaking loaded. Start off with defensive end Reggie White, an eventual Hall of Famer. Then there's defensive tackle Jerome Brown, who probably would have been a Hall of Famer if he hadn't gotten killed in a car crash. Throw in Clyde Simmons and Mike Golic, two very good pros, and where the hell am I going to fit in? The rest of the defense was just as nasty, with guys like Seth Joyner, Al Harris, Andre Waters, and Wes Hopkins. These guys were bringing it. If Buddy had given a crap about actually building the offense, instead of letting Randall Cunningham just run around, the Eagles probably would have won three Super Bowls. But that wasn't Buddy's thing. Buddy was about defense.

I wasn't afraid to go play for them, but I was not going somewhere just to be a tackling dummy so they could protect the older guys while getting the offense ready. Yeah, I would have loved to be just down the Jersey Turnpike from my family and friends. How crazy would that have been? Well, probably no worse than it turned out, but it was tempting. Instead, I got a call from the Colts, who were coming off an 8–8 season and made this big trade to get George with the number-one pick. George was like this returning hero because he was from Indianapolis and originally went to Purdue. Never mind that the guy quit on Purdue, then was afraid to go to the University of Miami without being assured the starting job before ending up at Illinois. They also had Eric Dickerson at running back, so things were looking pretty decent there. The defense had a few pretty good players, but I knew I could make it.

You see, making the NFL is not about the draft or what people think of you. It's about what you think of yourself. That's why you see so many undrafted or low-round picks make it big in the league. Tony Romo was undrafted. So was Kurt Warner. Tom Brady was a sixth-round pick. Johnny Unitas? Ninth round. John Randle, another defensive tackle who made it the same year as me and who is now in the Hall of Fame, was undrafted. In 2010 this kid Antonio Garay—a defensive tackle just like me who grew up in New Jersey, I know his family really well—he came out of nowhere and played great for San Diego. The ironic part is, he wasn't really much of a kid. He was thirty years old that season, but the point is, he kept plugging away, never giving up. He was undrafted too and even bounced around with a few teams before he figured it all out, got an opportunity, and showed somebody what he could do. The Chargers ended up having the number-one overall defense in the league last season, and I believe a lot of it was because they had a guy like Garay in the middle.

It was just like that for me when I played on Baltimore's Super Bowl championship team in 2000. Yeah, we had some stud athletes like Ray Lewis, Chris McAlister, and Peter Boulware. But we also had plenty of grinders like me, Rob Burnett, and Michael McCrary. We were all either undrafted or low-round picks who made it because we were smart, we loved the game, and, what I believe is most important, we all had heart. We all had strong support from our families and friends, and that's how we treated each other, like family. If you ever meet Burnett or McCrary, you ask them about their dad or their mom. You'll see what I mean.

Sure, there are plenty of scouts and executives who can look out there and pick out the talented guys: the players, who can run fast and jump high. That's easy. It doesn't take a freaking genius to see that Deion Sanders is fast and athletic, maybe the greatest thing since sliced provolone. And you can figure out pretty quickly that he can cover just about any human being in the world. That's not hard to figure. But for the rest of the draft, trying to pick out who's going to be a great player isn't easy.

Here's what I mean: from 1990 to 2011, there were only six number-one picks who went on to win even one Super Bowl, and that includes Drew Bledsoe winning one as a backup to Brady. The only guy to get picked first in that time and win more Super Bowls than I did with Baltimore was Russell Maryland with Dallas (and those Cowboys teams were pretty loaded). Here's the other side: all the number-one picks who were flops, like George, Emtman, Dan Wilkinson, Ki-Jana Carter, Tim Couch, Courtney Brown, David Carr, and the granddaddy of them all, JaMarcus Russell. Yeah, some of those guys got hurt. But I'll put my injuries up against theirs, and I still made it. In fact, I started from day one until the day I retired after twelve years in the NFL.

I just needed the right place to get a shot. It was like being back in Little League and just wanting to get another chance to bat. That was Indianapolis. Of course, first I had to figure out where Indianapolis was. See, when my agent told me Indianapolis, I thought he said, "Annapolis," as in Annapolis, Maryland. I didn't know where NFL teams played. I knew the New York Giants and the Jets, but I'd only been west of New Jersey one time in my life, when I went to Iowa State to visit. I didn't know where Indianapolis was. Yeah, yeah, I know, I must have had a great geography teacher in high school. So, all the time that my agent is talking, I'm thinking, *Cool, I'll just drive down to Annapolis and play there.*

After my agent explained to me where Indy was, I called Randy Dixon, an offensive tackle my agent and I knew from Pitt. He was playing for the Colts, so I wanted to hear his evaluation. He said, "Listen, they have some defensive linemen, but they are not as good as you." The year before I got there, they took this guy Mitch Benson in the third round from Texas Christian, and they had Harvey Armstrong, a veteran guy who had a great career but was on his way out. He was thirty-one years old, and he retired after my rookie season, as it turned out. Okay, I'll take my chances against that kind of competition, even if nobody thinks I'm worth enough to draft.

The Colts gave me $1,000 to sign and a rookie salary of something like $75,000, with another $10,000 if I made the roster. The signing bonus was such a joke; I went out with a bunch of people in my town and drank my signing bonus. Indianapolis also added a little language in the contract, because God forbid the Colts might have had to pay me $85,000 if I got hurt. Nope, no way—the Colts added a little clause saying they didn't have to pay me a dime if I got hurt because of my knee problems in college.

Now, usually the way contracts work in the NFL for young players is there's a "split," especially for the late-round picks and undrafted guys who are on the real edge of making it or not. If you're a first-, second-, or third-round pick, you have a little leverage to get around this part of a deal. Basically, here's how it works: If you make the team, you get your full base salary, whatever it is. These days, if you make it as a rookie, the minimum contract is like $400,000. So you make the team, you're making $400,000 as your pay. Back when I was a rookie, it was $85,000.

If you get hurt, it's different. They put you on injured reserve, or whatever category they have, and you get less, like maybe only $200,000, half of the minimum. And that's what is commonly known as a "split" contract in the NFL. You have clauses like that all the time in NFL contracts because so many guys get injured along the way. In addition, one or two guys every year—particularly the guys who realize pretty quickly they don't have a chance to make it—start to fake injuries so they can stick around the team and keep getting paid, milking the system. Now that the money is so big, you see that happen a lot. But trust me when I tell you that teams play their games too. The whole split contract is just the beginning of the things that teams do. One of the classic tricks by a team is to take an injured guy out on the field just before cut-down day before the season and tell him, "We really need to see you run." Most of these guys are so nervous, and thinking they have to do something to make it, that they go run, even if they're not healthy. Meanwhile, the team is videotaping them. Later the team cuts them and then uses the tape to show that they were healthy enough to run, even if they had something like a messed-up knee.

Anyway, none of that meant shit to me. At this point, just give me a contract and give me a shot. Even though my salary back then was only $85,000 total, the Colts wanted to be completely protected in case I got hurt again. So the clause for the split in my deal wasn't a split at all. It was truly get paid or get nothing. All these years later, you can see how it ended up.

This all goes back to this little working-class house and that weekend when everybody in the NFL passed on me, again and again and again. You have no idea how agonizing that was. This was my dream. This was what I'd thrown my whole life into. When I was a little kid, I couldn't play football because I was too big. I was on the team and I could practice, but I couldn't play, not until I got to high school. Now I was being told the same thing, over and over—I couldn't play. I wasn't good enough. I wasn't worth taking a chance on with a second-round pick, or a third or a fifth or an eighth or a twelfth. I'm surrounded by people who have supported me all the way from when I was a little kid, so it's like they're being told that everything they did wasn't worth a shit. From my mother making macaroni for every kid in the neighborhood, or my dad working three jobs and waking up in the middle of the night to make sandwiches for us when we came in from hanging out, or the cop who once taught me a lesson by not taking me in after I got caught buying alcohol under age, or all the people from the Italian-American Club, or the school, or the coaches, or everybody else who chipped in.

Well, to hell with all those NFL experts and coaches and personnel guys who passed on me. When I finally got my shot, the NFL got a guy with a serious chip on his shoulder. A big chip loaded with not only his own emotions, but what his family and friends felt too. It was just like when I was twelve years old and I swung at that pitch with everything I had. When I got my chance, I gave the NFL everything I had.

I remember during the first four or five years of my NFL career I used that same emotion all the time. I kept track of every coach who didn't pick me and kept saying, *I'm going to prove them wrong.* Every time we played against a coach who had passed on me, after the game I went up and shook his hand and said, "How ya doing, coach, remember me?" I made them all remember. Sometimes during the game, if I got close to the sideline, I would look for one of those guys who put me through all that misery. I wanted to get real close and let them all know. That was the fire that burned inside me to prove everybody wrong. I would say to myself, *This guy doesn't think I was good enough to draft? All right, here we go.*

02

JERSEY BOY

If you want to understand my crazy, risk-taking way of living, my willingness to take chances, knowing all the while that I'll be okay even if things don't work out, you have to start in Kenilworth, this little dot of a town in northern New Jersey. Yeah, I have the "do it yourself" confidence, but that comes from some pretty strong roots.

I was born in Kenilworth, a two-square-mile borough that seemed like it was 99 percent Italian. My mother used to stand on the back steps and yell, "Anthony!" and twenty kids would come running. We had pasta for every meal. Mom would make four pounds of macaroni, and we'd all just go at it. My dad, Pete Siragusa Sr., had a few jobs over the years. He worked for General Dynamics as a tool-and-die maker, and then he drove a cement truck during the week and a limousine on weekends. Eventually, my folks opened up an Italian restaurant, which is one reason why

I have a bunch of restaurants now. It's in my blood, what can I say? My old man, he worked seven days a week. Us kids, we worked on weekends too. There was always just enough money to scrape by, to give everyone three pairs of corduroys and a couple of iron-on CHARLIE'S ANGELS T-shirts for school. A couple of summers the family saved up, and we would drive down to Florida, only instead of taking us three or four days like a normal family, it would take us almost a week to get there because my two brothers and me would end up fighting in the back of our station wagon and my dad would turn the car around. We'd drive back a good hundred miles before my mom got my dad calmed down and he'd head south again. It was good times.

A lot of people in Jersey talk about going to the beach in summertime like that's all people from around here ever do. When I was growing up, we would go down to Wildwood, down by Cape May, for one week every summer. My dad would save up money all year for that one week. That was a real treat, but we were on a budget. We'd go to the boardwalk for one night, and that was it, no big spending. I barely knew what sand was when I was growing up. Now we have a freaking beach house where I take my kids every summer, and we stay there the whole time, unless we're traveling somewhere else. It's ridiculous. Video games? We had an air hockey game in the garage and built potato launchers with PVC pipe when I was a kid. We didn't have a freaking PlayStation or whatever they got now. But you know what, it was great. I didn't know what I didn't have, so I had no idea what we were supposedly missing.

Part of our routine was the train that used to run through town to the old Monsanto plant. The tracks ran right next to my family's house back then (they're gone now, just like Monsanto), and then by the Little League field on the way to the plant, where who knows what they were making. Monsanto was seriously secretive about what was going on in that place. They had their own security force around that place 24/7. There were the Kenilworth cops, guys you knew and could joke around with. Then there were the Monsanto cops, who were like FBI. No screwing around for those guys. I have no idea what Monsanto was building in there, but they made sure nobody was going to find out.

If it had been the local cops in charge, they would have given us a tour of the place. Better yet, when we had buddies working at other places, it was a party. Schering-Plough Pharmaceuticals was here before getting bought out by Merck. I had a buddy who was a security guard for Schering-Plough. He had all the keys to the place, including one to the CEO's office. My buddy knew where all the good stuff was, so every now and then we'd help ourselves to a couple of bottles for some cocktails. When you have cocktails, you have to have something to eat, so we'd hit the kitchen next. It was our own private country club. The best part was no dues. I would enjoy a couple of Taylor hams. Of course, we would never clean up after ourselves, but the people who ran the kitchen never ratted us out.

Anyway, the train only came through once a day, and we'd jump on it as it meandered through town. We knew the conductors, so it was cool. Then we'd jump off, and we'd all play baseball or stickball or whatever we felt like. Nowadays, kids can't have a game unless they have every parent, the nanny, three refs, and sixteen coaches per team. It's ridiculous. Most of the kids I coach, they don't even really know the rules. When we were kids, you had to know the rules because there were no refs most of the time, no umpires. If we didn't have a rule, we made it up. That was the great thing about playing with all your buddies, and half the time that's what you got into a fight about. You'd be arguing about whether the ball was fair or foul and pretty soon you were brawling. No problem, you work right through that shit. That's what made us all so tight.

My friends from growing up, we're tight to this day. When you grow up in a small community of guys, obviously you fought with each other, but no one ever messed with us. That's because if you messed with one of us, you messed with all of us. I was as tight with the guys in my town as I was with my brothers. To this day, if I was in trouble, I could call ten or twenty guys right now, and they'd be here as fast as they could. They would drop everything. We're talking about serious loyalty, something that's really hard to find these days. There's one phone call made, and there are fifty guys in the high school parking lot with baseball bats going, "Where are they?" That's how I grew up. I didn't know any better, and I took that to the football field. With a football team, that's what you're trying to achieve. You have to have that camaraderie that goes all the way to, "Listen, you mess with my guys on the field, I'm going to kill you." I took everything very personally, and that helped me become a professional football player.

It wasn't just the kids who were like that. Kenilworth has very serious pride in its school system. We used to be in a regional school system with a total of seven towns. When the population went down, the school system tried to close down our school. The people here got pissed and said, no way. Instead of closing the school, Kenilworth seceded from the regional school system. I think the board and the school system didn't know who they were messing with when they screwed with us. You weren't supposed to be able to do that, but this little town forced the state to let them out, and we formed our own prekindergarten-through-twelfth-grade system.

Of course, Kenilworth was a very family-oriented town, but there were other families that were represented who we just didn't talk about. Yeah, you maybe knew who the bookies were, but you always respected every elder in town because you never knew. My dad and grandfather always impressed that on me—to respect everybody because you never know who somebody might be. The best way to think about it is this phrase: life is a fragile thing. When we were really young, you didn't know that the black van with the tinted windows parked down the street was anything special. By the time you were eleven or twelve, you knew that was the FBI checking on somebody. Trust me, any new car around town, we immediately knew. It was almost stupid for the feds to even hang out in our town because everybody knew and everybody talked. Somebody would see a van or a new car, and all of a sudden there's twenty phone calls being made.

Trust me, I'm not making this stuff up. It doesn't take a freaking genius to know we've had our share of connected guys. I was a toddler when they convicted Simone "Sam the Plumber" DeCavalcante. He ran mob operations all over New Jersey. The front business for his operations? Kenilworth Heating and Air Conditioning. Yeah, that was back in 1969. Trust me, things haven't changed much. In 2011 you could read headlines like these:

"NJ Mafia Busts Made by FBI in Edison and Kenilworth"
"Quiet Kenilworth Neighborhood Sees Arrest of Soldier in the
    Genovese Crime Family, Three Others in Organized Crime
    Sweep"
"Alleged Mob Member from Kenilworth to Appear at Bail
    Hearing"

Stuff like that was a regular part of my youth. We had the head of the Teamsters, Frank Carracino, investigated in our town. They found a guy with bodies down in a subbasement, where they would cut them up to get rid of them. The stuff is crazy. I can't make this up. Whenever there was an indictment in New York City, they'd come to our town to start rounding people up. My butcher got indicted. The guy who made shoes, he got indicted. Something big would happen, and all of a sudden the Italian-American Club down the street was half-empty. Even now, that's true. Just a few months ago, they swept in and got six or seven guys from my town. That was just the kind of life we had.

When I finally got to the NFL, the FBI came in and laid out a bunch of pictures. They were of people I knew from town. They even had pictures of me sitting with different guys. I'm looking and saying, "Yeah, that's my neighbor." I'm not saying any names. Maybe I would say, "That guy is a friend of the family or whatever." The FBI would tell me, "Oh, he's a made guy in an organized crime family." It's like what you hear from some of the guys on the team who grew up in hard-core neighborhoods. The feds come in and tell you to stay away, but it's not that easy. These are people you grew up with.

When people see a mob guy, they think about the movie image. There are some guys like that, like John Gotti, all flashy, pimped out with the big suits and the big black Cadillacs. Those guys don't last long. Really, it's the little old man who lives in the brick house down the street in the blue-collar town. All of a sudden there's an indictment, and you see fifteen cars in front of the guy's house with the lights flashing. They search the house for the money, but don't find it until they look in the car and they find $250,000. Of course, it's a rental car, so the feds can't prosecute him. Who is this guy? I knew him as somebody completely different. A guy like that, who you've known since you were a little kid, it's like he's hiding in plain sight. The FBI guys are looking at me saying, "You can't be hanging out with this guy, or this guy, or this guy . . . this guy is a bookie, that guy is a hit man." It was a real eye-opener. I almost figured I couldn't go home anymore. But this is home; this is where I grew up. I can't walk away from that.

And Kenilworth is a place you always come back to. These days my mom splits her time between there and Florida, and my oldest brother Pete still lives in the last house we lived in. Sure, I don't live there anymore, but I don't live far away. I'm about twenty minutes away, and the only reason I'm not in Kenilworth is because there's no place where you can buy an acre or two and have a big backyard with some woods the way I do now. That doesn't exist in Kenilworth because it's a town of working-class people. That's what it says right on the sign to the town, WELCOME TO KENILWORTH, AN "INDUSTRIAL CITY." The word *city* is a little much when you talk about Kenilworth. Not only is it a good bike ride from one end to the other, it's all of 8,000 people. When I was a kid back in the early 1970s, we were booming with about 9,000 people. There are some Italian weddings with more people than my hometown.

Of all those people, I probably know at least half of them personally. I might not remember their names anymore—you try remembering a bunch of stuff after you've spent your life slamming your head into another human being . . . or six. I've got some memory loss from football, but that's another story. As for the people I grew up with, I know them. I may not remember everything, but I know we played football together, or went to school together, or went to church together. Or I know their cousin who worked with my cousin and did a thing for that guy over there. When I graduated from David Brearley High School in 1985, my class had 175 people. I still see those people all the time. That's how it works in Kenilworth—everybody does for each other because it's all blue-collar people. This guy is an electrician, and that guy is a plumber. This guy works at the auto repair place, so they all do something for somebody. You need your car fixed? Do you go to the shop? Forget about it, the mechanic comes to you on Saturday because he's probably your second cousin once removed or your neighbor. You need some drywall put up because you're remodeling (or you're fixing the wall from the party that got out of control)? You call over four or five guys, and the drywall probably fell off a truck. Everybody helps everybody. That's how I grew up, and I wouldn't change it for anything in the world.

If you drive around the town, you can see right away what I'm talking about. There are lots of little working-class homes. Don't take that the wrong way—most everybody takes care of their stuff. The yards are clean, the houses are kept up, you don't see a lot of beat-up cars up on blocks on the lawn or nothing like that. But you also don't see any big ranch-style houses with the big yard all the way around. If you have 2,500 square feet in Kenilworth, you're living large. Most houses are somewhere between 1,000 and 1,500 square feet. See, that's another cool thing about Kenilworth. Pretty much everybody is on the same level. You don't have all these rich people looking down their noses at anybody, and you don't have a lot of people with a cup in their hand. Really, Kenilworth is like a giant family. When I was growing up, I probably could tell you who 90 percent of the people were in the houses.

Of course, that works two ways, and here's my first story about that. When I was in high school, we used to have parties for the team out on the golf course just down the block from my house. We'd get a keg and some wine. I was the biggest guy on the team, so when it was time to buy the Boone's Farm wine for the team party (you know, that really cheap stuff you get for like $2 a bottle), I was pretty much the guy to get it done. So I'm at the liquor store, this place we used to call "the Old Homestead." I get like three bottles of wine, and I come strolling out. All of a sudden, here comes one of the cops, William Dowd, and he stops me right there in front of this place. He looks at me and says, "What the hell are you doing?" I'm standing there, caught red-handed. I say, "Oh, come on, man," but he takes the bottles and starts saying, "You're in trouble, you're going to jail, get in the back of the car." I'm like, "All right, take me to jail." I'm acting a little like a cocky asshole. So then Dowd, who later became the chief of police in Kenilworth, thinks about it for a second and says, "No, I'm taking you home."

What? What are you talking about, you're going to take me home?! My dad is home. No, no, no way. He says, "Yeah, I'm taking you home. I'm pulling up in front of your house, and I'm putting the sirens on." I start crying, "Don't take me home, take me to jail, it's the law." Dowd fires back at me: "Don't you tell me the law." He knows because he knows my dad. He knows that if he pulls up with the sirens blaring, I'm toast. My dad is going to beat my ass. But Dowd keeps talking it up. "I'm putting the sirens on, the lights on, and I'm walking you to the front door." I pleaded with him, I said, "I will never drink again the rest of my life, please." I'm begging and begging. If he puts on the sirens and the lights, I'm going to piss myself in fear because I know I'm gonna get a beating. He pulled up in front of my house, and I was like, "Please!" Dowd gets out, gets me out of the back of the car, and brings me halfway up the walkway. Then he says, "All right, I'm going to cut you a break, but if I ever catch you buying alcohol or drinking again. . . . "

I'm like, "Thank you, thank you," totally in a panic. Don't worry about me drinking again. I think I stayed in the house for three weeks, I wouldn't even leave. My buddies would call and say, "Hey, man, can you make it over? We're having a party." I was like, to hell with that. There was lots of other stuff like that. You go around town, it's like you got eight hundred sets of parents. You do something stupid, either some adult is going to call your folks and let them know or they'll come out and take care of it themselves. If you complain to your parents about what some-body else's folks did, you're liable to get another beatin' yourself for doing something in the first place and then for complaining about it. Every-body is tight, and everybody looks after everybody else. You don't see that in other communities anymore because too many people are thinking about only themselves.

My old man was special. I'm going to talk about him some more later, but let me give you a brief description right now. Pete Siragusa Sr. was one tough nut. Probably about five-foot-nine or five-foot-ten and about three hundred pounds. He was built solid, like a freaking fire hydrant. When he was young, he used to sing and play in a band around New Jersey. That's how he met my mom. He was playing in the band, and she was one of the dancers who came along. Of course, you listen to my mom and she'll tell you that it was my dad who chased her. She talks about how she wouldn't give him the time of day for a long while, until he really begged her to go out with him. I don't know, I wasn't there, but I'll go with what my mom is saying. My dad passed away when I was in college; he had a heart attack right in the house in the middle of the night. I'll get back to that a little later, but suffice to say, he was special. He wasn't afraid to work or get up in front of people to perform. In my case, the apple doesn't fall far from the tree. When we'd get back home at night, he'd come out to the kitchen and fix us something to eat, make sure everybody was okay.

As for my mom, you gotta remember, when we were growing up, she was the toughest lady you've ever seen. To hear me tell stories about her, you would think she has a little mole on her neck with hair coming out of it, like the old Italian lady dressed in black. Having three sons, especially the three of us, I don't know how she did it. You have to know that my mother is one of those women who doesn't just cook for one or two peo-ple. You come over to her house for lunch, she doesn't just cook a couple of meatballs. She's making like fifty meatballs and a big dish of macaroni. It was like that in high school all the time. We would have a couple of guys show up, and then a couple more. She was feeding people all the time. It was endless. She had this standard 48-inch, round dining table, but then we would add four leaves to it and it'd be like 127 inches. We'd have fourteen or fifteen people around the table, and we always were putting the leaves in. Every day each of us would bring in some friends, and there was always food. My mom was working every minute to take care of us. It was like she was hosting a dinner party every night, except we weren't exactly high-class guests with all our buddies. To this day, my mother doesn't pay for anything around town. She never even pays to get her taxes done, because she took care of so many kids along the way.

My mother went to every wrestling match and every other event we had. My father would come to every one that he could, but he had to work. Football, wrestling, baseball, I don't know how she did it. We had a little car. We didn't have a truck, no Suburban to haul us around and all our stuff. We just jumped in the car, and she got us where we needed to go. Plus, my mom knows her stuff when it comes to sports. By the time the three of us were done with wrestling, she could have coached college wrestling. She knew every move there was. She'd be screaming instructions because she'd been to so many wrestling matches. In football, she'd cook with the other moms. She did everything, and it was amazing. And what's more amazing is that you see her now and she looks great. People meet my mom and then they look at me. Then they look back at her and look back at me. They get that funny look on their face and say, "That's not your mom. She's too pretty and too young-looking."

My mom did a damn good job as a wrestling coach. My oldest brother Pete, who still lives in Kenilworth, he was probably the best of all of us, but he could never make the state championships because he had some unbelievable wrestlers in his class, the 158-pound class. When I was in high school, I was in the heavyweight class, and we had some great athletes, future NFL players like Lester Archambeau, Keith Sims, and Dave Szott. That's four guys who each played at least ten years in the NFL. Talk about some tough guys. Of course, I pinned them all.

Before I get too cocky, let me say that I wasn't always a great wrestler. As I said before, I was good when I was young, not great. I got my ass kicked a lot in wrestling. I always went against bigger kids. One day I was just like, "I'm tired of this shit. I'm not getting pinned anymore." Something went off in my head, and I became a wacko and never lost again. I don't know what happened, I just got pissed, and competing against guys like that in high school helped me so much when I played football. Learning about leverage and hand placement—that stuff was all invaluable to playing football at the higher levels.

My younger brother, Elio, now there's a tough guy too. He was a heavyweight also. He finished second in the state and did that after breaking his ankle in the semifinals. He won that match with a broken ankle and then competed in the championships. He would have won if he wasn't hurt. He couldn't even stand up.

When I was in high school, there was no *Friday Night Lights.* We didn't even have lights on our field when I was a kid, and we played our high school games on Saturday. You remember that Tom Cruise movie *All the Right Moves,* from 1983? That was back when I was a teenager. Cruise's character is from this Pennsylvania steel town. When the team plays, the whole town just shuts down. If you were a crook, you could have robbed every house and business in our town on Saturday when we were playing. It was all about football. Everybody would go to the game. When we played Pop Warner, that was on Sunday, and we used to go to Mass at 7:00 A.M. A lot of guys would go in their shoulder pads. Most of us were

Catholic, so it wasn't something we were going to miss. Some of the guys would even ride over on their bikes. After Mass, all the moms would cook breakfast for us.

What's funny is, my Pop Warner coach was actually one of the first people to give me the motivation to keep playing. My Pop Warner coach was Bill Chango, a great man, but a guy I used to mouth off to way too much. I would always bust his chops at practice, even though I was over-weight and couldn't play a lot of the time. One day he came up to me and said, "Listen, you should find something else to do. You'll never make it playing football." He didn't exactly say I was horrible, but he might as well have. That gave me a big dose of fire in my belly, because I wanted to prove him wrong so bad. That was rough, but Chango made up for it later.

Our high school coach was Bob Taylor. If he told you to do some-thing, it got done. It's not like now, where some kids don't listen to their coaches, and some even talk back to them. Coach Taylor had the com-plete backing of our parents. If he went to your dad and said, "Hey, Tony ain't listening to me," it was like, holy shit, you're in deep. There wasn't some time-out to go sit. The only time-out was when your dad was done beating your ass. That's how it was.

Usually, our school was really good in football. Both my brothers played on undefeated teams. My team wasn't nearly that good, but we would fight you like hell. I played left tackle on offense and this combo middle linebacker/noseguard position on defense. I was like an extra de-fensive lineman standing up over the center instead of down in a stance. They triple-teamed me all the time with the center and the two guards. That was fun. I also punted and kicked for us, so I never came off the field. When I got to college and only played defense, all I thought was, *This is easy.*

When I was getting recruited by colleges, the coaches would all show up for my wrestling meets. That was a show. We had Lou Holtz and Jimmy Johnson up in the stands, all these other coaches. I would go on recruiting trips, but I could never stay for the whole weekend like the other recruits because I had to come back for the meets. After I went down to Miami, I came back to this meet against New Providence High wearing my black leather jacket. Everybody is asking me how it went. I take off the jacket, weigh in for my match, and then go pin my guy. It was pretty sweet.

In fact, my entire school and Pop Warner career happened on one field. The elementary school and the middle school where I went were right on the same property as the high school. In fact, this whole piece of land was part of my mother's family farm way back when. My grandfather had all of it, and it was wide open until they started building up the town.

When we played Pop Warner, the coach used to run us like hell, really beat us up pretty good at practice. He kept the key to the water spigot on a chain around his neck. If we did a really good job, he would give us the key to the spigot for three minutes. We had to run to the spigot, turn it on, and get as much water as we could in that one break. That was it, one break. Now they have every sports drink in the world, G2, G3, G8, whatever it is. It's unbelievable. We had nothing.

When I donate money to David Brearley High School, it's always in my dad's name. The football field is Pete Siragusa Field. The wrestling room is now named after him. I go back to my school once in a while and see that a lot of things have changed with the times. The doors aren't open like they were when I was a kid. We used to hang out on one side of the school most of the time, just outside the locker room, where there's a big double door out to the parking lot. Everybody came through there all day long, and we'd check everybody out. I can't tell you how many guys I stuffed in a locker over the years. Not the nicest thing in the world, but what the hell. One day I went to the auto shop class, got a saw, and then sawed the wall between my locker and the next one over so I had a double locker.

Across the hall from the locker room was the weight room. When I was in school, there was a full-size picture of William "The Refrigerator" Perry on the wall. He was four hundred pounds or something and tearing up the NFL at the time with those great Chicago Bears teams. Most kids would look at that and get intimidated. I'd look at it and say, "One day that's going to be me." They also had the beautician classes down the hall, where the girls were learning to cut hair and stuff, so we would hang out there all the time too. I'd say, "Hey, I just need a little trimming up," then I'd spend like an hour in there.

The trophy cases and the Wall of Fame are all there. There's stuff from when I won the state title in wrestling. There's a trophy with my wife Kathy's score in gymnastics (her maiden name is Giacalone). She still has the highest score ever in the all-around for our school. My picture on the Wall of Fame, that's a beauty. There's like nine people on there, all of them dressed up nice, looking sharp—guys in suits and ties and all that. Then there's me, on the sideline in a Ravens game with sunglasses on at the end of the game because we blew somebody out. You know what? Nobody said a word when that was the picture I sent in, because that's how they all know me.

The other thing is that people remember that I really cared about that school, just like I care about the town to this day. When I was in school, we had these two old Italian guys who were the janitors. They both spoke broken English. We used to go over there in the morning and make coffee for those guys, try to help them out a little. But we had these dirtbag kids at the school who were trashing the place every day. So I was a junior at the time, but I got aggravated and told the principal, "This is ridiculous." Then I went over and got all those kids who made the mess and said: "Start cleaning up. You expect the janitors to pick up after you? That's bullshit, they aren't your mothers, clean up after yourself." I made them get brooms and clean the whole school. After that, all the students did a better job of picking up. You have to have a little pride.

Anyway, a little while later, I got called into the office, and I was thinking, *Shit, what did I do wrong? What are they going to suspend me for?* The principal said, "Oh, by the way, you're student of the month, the first one ever." They actually started this award because of me. I wasn't trying to kiss ass, I was just telling these guys that they were being jerks because they were. I didn't give a damn. I did it because this was our place, our school. I did it because I love this place. Maybe that's why I'm the only guy with two keys to the city: the mayor gave me one, and then they gave me another one when they had a parade for me one time. This place has been in my heart forever. When I got married, after I had already been in the NFL for a while, I didn't big-time it and go to New York City or something like that for the bachelor party. We all went to Billy Buffy's, the neighborhood bar. We rented the whole place out and had a great time. . . . I'll leave it at that.

I did it because this all means something to me. Back then and all the way to today.

GOOSE TALES WITH . . .
MOTHER GOOSE

Rosemarie Siragusa is the mother of Pete Jr., Anthony, and Elio Siragusa. She splits her time between New Jersey, where she and her late husband, Pete Sr., raised the three boys, and Florida, where she is trying to recuperate from her children.

"When Tony—I called him Anthony when he was growing up—was young, you could never let him out of your sight, not for a minute. Every time I took my eyes off him, he was getting hurt, running into something, falling off this, trying to unlock the front door. The nurses at the emergency room knew him by his first name. They'd see him and say, 'Oh, Tony, what is it this time?' He wasn't a bad boy. He just could never sit still.

"He also tried to get out of doing things all the time, tried to find a way around it. When he was about seven or eight years old, my husband looked at him and said, 'Why don't you rake the lawn, do something to clean up?' We're just sitting out in front of the house, watching out over the neighborhood. At the time, my husband had this little scooter, kind of a minibike. I didn't like it because I always thought one of the boys would get hurt. All of a sudden, here comes Tony around the house on the scooter with the rake tied to the back of it. This is how he was going to rake the lawn. We're laughing, but then I tell my husband that I'm worried. He says, 'Oh, don't worry, he'll be fine.' Well, of course, Tony eventually falls over on the minibike, the sprocket where the chain is attached puts a big hole in his leg, and we're off to the emergency room. 'Oh, Tony, what is it this time?'

"Another time, when my youngest son Elio was still just a baby or a toddler, we were at the park. I'm holding Elio, and I take my eyes off Tony for a second. He was in the playground, and all of a sudden one of the other mothers brings him over to me, and he's got blood all over him. 'Tony, what happened?' He said he walked behind the swings and one of the bolts on the swing caught him right on the forehead. He still has the scar from that one. He has scars all over his body.

"Another time, same kind of thing, my husband was coaching Tony in football. He never showed the boys any favoritism, so this one time he made Tony run a lap for something. Well, Tony starts running, and he gets hit by some kid on a bike, and now he has this big hole in the back of his leg. Really tore up the back of his leg. He must have been about nine at the time. My husband grabbed him and carried him all the way to the car and drove him to the hospital. 'Oh, Tony, what is it this time?' The kid was a walking accident, an accident waiting to happen. He still has a big scar on the back of his leg from that one.

"He was just a menace. Not a discipline problem, just never sitting still for one second. He started walking when he was ten months old, and he even started climbing out of the crib. My husband had to lower the crib so he wouldn't fall out and break his head. The other thing he'd do was move the crib. We lived in this two-family [duplex] house when the kids were young, until we built the house we ended up in. The way the two-family was built, it had a long hallway that led to one of the three bedrooms. That was Tony's room when he was a baby. We put his crib at one end of the room, but it was on wheels, so eventually he learned to move it by swaying back and forth and getting it rolling. He'd roll it to the end of the room, where he could look down the hall and see us. Then he'd hold up his bottle and yell, 'More!' That kid must have gone through three or four bottles every time. My husband used to call him 'Bam Bam' after the baby on *The Flintstones.* He looked just like that: a cute, chubby kid. He was nine pounds, eleven ounces when he was born.

"And he would never sleep, which meant I was always tired. This one time, he climbed out of his crib and came to the bedroom where I was sleeping. All I wanted was two more minutes, just a little more rest. So I held his hand to keep him close to me, like an alarm clock in case he tried to let go and go somewhere. Finally I wake up and find that he has a steak knife in his other hand and he's poking holes in the box spring. My box spring looks like Swiss cheese. He must have gone in the kitchen and gotten the knife. Oh my God, he could have hurt himself or killed me. This kid, he was unbelievable.

"The other thing he'd do all the time was try to open the front door to go outside. He didn't want to run away, he just wanted to see what was out there. He couldn't have been much more than a year old, and he'd move a chair to the front door, climb up on it, and try to turn the knob. My husband had to put a hook at the top of the door to keep him from going outside. Oh, the stories with that one."

03

GOOD FIGHTS
AND BAD KNEES

As I was going through the recruiting process coming out of high school, the whole thing unfolded a lot easier than you might expect. As I mentioned before, I had a lot of major colleges and coaches showing interest in me. Guys like Lou Holtz, who was in the middle of going from Minnesota to Notre Dame, and Jimmy Johnson, who was at the University of Miami at the time, would show up at my wrestling meets. Back then, there weren't any of the restrictions that you have now, where head coaches can't really go that much. It didn't matter that we were on the East Coast; this was the wild, wild West of recruiting. They'd come to my house and start talking. Some of those guys had no clue what they were doing when they were talking to my parents. You'd get some coaches from the South who would always say, "And we have some nice-looking girls on our campus." My dad didn't want to hear any of that shit. He'd be really nice about it, though. He'd smile and basically say, "That's good, now take your cannoli and go."

Like I said, there were no guidelines back then. I'd get calls all the time, like 250 letters a day, banners, pennants, hats, T-shirts, all sorts of shit. My whole room was covered in posters, even the ceiling. I had all these schools chasing me, so it was pretty cool. When it came time to visit schools, I narrowed it down to a handful before I made up my mind. Some schools did a good job of eliminating themselves. For instance, Notre Dame was pretty funny. One of the coaches from there called me up at one point and started saying, "We've heard about you, and you're going to have to change your ways a little if you want to play for Notre Dame." They wanted me to come, but I was a little rough around the edges for them, and this guy was giving me a lecture. I was like, "Thank you very much for helping me make my decision," and I hung up on him.

My first stop was in Miami, and it's hard to beat that place for a good time. Of course, the Hurricanes were in the middle of building their glory years with guys like Vinny Testaverde and Jerome Brown and those studs they had at the time. For me, though, there was no way I could do it. Look, it was the '80s, and I knew if I went there, trouble wasn't lurking, it would find me. I couldn't afford to waste college on that. I went to a couple of parties. I didn't realize until then that it snows in Miami. If I had gone down there, this would have been the last chapter of my book. On top of that, there was Johnson with his fake-ass hair. Now Jimmy and I work together at FOX, and I bust his balls all the time about this. I love the guy now, but back then, as he was sitting there and telling me why I should come to the University of Miami and all this other shit, all I was thinking was, *How long does it take for him to do his hair?* Then I was thinking, *Is his head a fire hazard from all the hair-care products?* I'm thinking to myself, *This guy is full of it. Don't be trying to BS me, don't bullshit a bullshitter.* He's talking about how I might play if I come down there. *Dude, I'm playing and I'm going to kick ass.*

Then came the biggest con man I ever met, Frank D'Alonzo, who was recruiting for Iowa State at the time. Now, this was shaping up like a good deal. They flew me to Ames, Iowa, where the school is located, on this private Gulfstream jet with D'Alonzo after he came to see me wrestle. This was an awesome way to travel. This was like a $40 million jet or something like that. I was thinking, *I have to get me one of these.* But as we got close to Ames, I got my first weird feeling about Iowa State. D'Alonzo handed me scuba gloves and this neoprene headgear. Seriously, it was all that neoprene stuff you wear when you go diving, but there was no water anywhere in sight. This was the first time I'd been west of New Jersey in my life, and suddenly I was thinking, *What the hell is this?* Well, it was the dead of winter in Iowa, and it felt like it was 75 below when I got off the plane.

Are you out of your freaking mind? Now, it got better when I saw a busload of sorority girls there to pick me up and escort me around. That was good. Then, as we drove through the middle of Ames, D'Alonzo pointed out this Corvette in the middle of a parking lot with a bow on it. He asked me what I thought. I nodded and said, "That's sweet." D'Alonzo said right back, "If you come to Iowa State, that could be yours."

So I went on with the girls. We ended up going snowmobiling, which I had never done before. At one point, all I remember is sitting in a barber's chair and having about twenty shots poured down my throat. That trip was so great that I never even made it to campus. Too bad the place was way too cold and way too far away, even if I was going to get a

Corvette. So I left and told them, "Yeah, okay, I'll let you know." At least that way they sent me back home on the private jet.

I had another visit to Boston College. I kind of went there as a favor to my uncle Marty Sica, because Jack Bicknell was coaching there at the time. Bicknell had been my uncle's coach in high school in New Jersey, so I kind of felt obligated, and my dad really wanted me to go there. I actually almost did go because my trip was awesome. I loved Boston and BC. The only problem was that the school made all the players stay in a freshman dorm together the first year, and I wasn't into that at all. I'm a man of the people, you know, and I wasn't going to follow any rules like that.

My next visit was to West Virginia. That was a little wacky. I went to the place, and I was waiting in this room when two white guys with Mohawks and flannel shirts showed up. *What the hell is this? Did I just land in a remake of* Deliverance? We went out around the campus and the whole place was a little weird. The campus seemed like it was literally surrounded by a trailer park. The trailers were everywhere. We ended up in this area called "Sunnyside," which was part of the campus. The cool thing about West Virginia was that the fans were totally into it. You'd walk by these fans and they'd literally start screaming at you. They were like crazy dedicated. But then I ended up seeing the strangest thing ever. I was looking out on the campus, and I saw this dog with horns, and it scared the shit out of me. I thought it was some kind of freaking alien. I was like, *What the hell is that dog with horns?* They said to me, "That's a deer." What the hell? I'm from New Jersey; you don't see deer in Kenilworth.

Another visit I had was an unofficial deal to Penn State with my parents. We went up for their spring game, and it was just the three of us: me, my father, and my mother. Everybody up there was very nice, very cool. We were checking it out, and people were outside the stadium in their RVs, having a good time. But it didn't take long to notice that they had this big pasture of cows right next to the stadium and the whole place smelled like cow shit. All I could smell the whole time was cow shit; it was crazy. I was just thinking, *Oh my God, I can't smell anything but manure.* It got overwhelming. Of course, Joe Paterno was a good guy when we met him, but the whole place was a little over the top for me. Kind of like a cult. Little did I know what we would all find out years later. Afterward, there was a little get-together for all the guys from Pennsylvania and New Jersey, and I was seriously thinking about taking an official visit later on. But the whole time the people from Penn State weren't giving us anything: no water, no cookies, nothing. Those were the rules—kids and parents weren't supposed to get anything—and so at one point my dad got charged $1 for a couple of cookies. All I remember is that I started to get really aggravated about how cheap Penn State was being. I know there are rules, but there's also a little common sense. I was just thinking to myself, *You're going to charge my dad for cookies?* Right after that, I told my dad: "These guys can kiss my ass. They want me to come here, and I'm going to make millions of dollars for them, but you have to pay a dollar for cookies? To hell with that." Penn State was going to be on television and make all that money, and they couldn't find a way to give out a few cookies?

I was so pissed, because my father worked so hard for his money. He scratched and saved for all of us, but they were going to jack him around for a buck. To hell with that.

Finally, I visited the University of Pittsburgh. I told them that I wanted to be at a place where my dad could afford to come and see a game. He couldn't do that in Miami or Iowa, and I realized that family was too important for me to go anywhere too far away. Pittsburgh seemed like just the right distance—it was about a five-hour drive. Coach Foge Fazio seemed like a good guy—he had a vowel at the end of his name, which was good by me—and he was just weird enough that I thought he'd keep things interesting. I liked all the players too. Plus, when we went out to a bar called Peter's Pub during my recruiting visit, some loudmouth came in and started messing with one of the players. All the guys on the team had his back. It was awesome; those guys had the same values that I grew up with. It was like being back in Kenilworth. I made up my mind: I was going to Pitt.

One thing you have to know about Pittsburgh, it's really, truly, a tough-guy town. Actually, not just guys—the broads are tough too. If you can't fight, you don't survive. So I got in a lot of fights. People would come into the bar, or wherever you were, and say, "Hey, who's the toughest guy in the place?" *Boom*, next thing you know I'm brawling. It was survival; that's all I knew. With that as the backdrop, my brothers and some high school friends used to come visit me on weekends, or whenever we all had a break. We made a lot of crazy memories when they rolled into town. This is one of the best ones.

My brothers and I went out to a bar called Decade one weekend when I was at Pitt. The three of us are there, and Elio and I are standing by the bar. This is the first time Elio, who's probably about seventeen at the time, has gone out drinking with us, so all of a sudden he's buying drinks for everybody, having a good time, and I'm laughing. Pete's also a little lit up, he goes a little bananas when he starts drinking, but it's no big deal for now, and he heads over to the dance floor, which is on this slightly different level than the bar. Pete is wearing some ugly-ass yellow shirt, and suddenly I see a flash of yellow out of the corner of my eye. When a fight breaks out on the dance floor, I immediately think Pete is getting the shit kicked out of him. So Elio and I spring into action. We jump in there, and the next thing you know, the entire place is full of men and women punching, kicking, biting, scratching, throwing stuff—it's crazy.

It isn't until all hell has broken loose that I realize it's some other guy and not Pete who has been getting pounded. Oh well, too late now. Of course, Pete is now fighting too, because he saw me fighting. Man, did we screw this one up.

Anyway, during the middle of this whole thing, someone jumps on my back and starts grabbing my hair and is pulling it out of my scalp. I had a mullet at the time, and my hair was kind of long. So I get the person off me and push them off to the side. I'm back fighting somebody, and this person comes back after me. My hair is getting pulled again. Thinking back, this person was probably just trying to save me from a bad hair day, but it didn't feel good. So I punch this person, who I can't even see. The place starts to clear out. One last guy gives me a sucker punch, and I chase him out the door. As I open the door, there's this guy on the other side with a gun. We're standing there, and he says, "Open your fucking mouth!" Oh shit. I open my mouth, and he puts the gun in my mouth, and he says, "You're going to die right now for fighting my friends." As he's doing this, he sprays my face with a can of mace, and that shit is burning me everywhere. Because my mouth is open, he hits my uvula. It swells up so bad that I can barely breathe. My tongue was still hanging out of my mouth the next day.

Luckily, down the street are some cops and they see the whole thing. This one cop has a Rottweiler and lets the dog go. The dog is running up and the cops are running up, so this guy puts the gun away and tries to flee, but the dog catches him and the cops grab him. They throw him in the paddy wagon. I'm all fucked up because of the mace, screaming for water or whatever I can get on me to stop the burning. By now, my brothers are there, and when things start to calm down, they're laughing their asses off at me. As it turns out, the person I hit was related to the guy with the gun. The next day the police contact me and ask if I want to press charges. I find out the guy's name and everything. But before I decide, I get a call from home in New Jersey. I'm told to not press charges, and I come to find out that the guy with the gun is connected. I mean, this is serious, the real-deal family-type stuff. Not the bullshit kind of mobster that Italian kids from Jersey all pretend to be when they're growing up, talking about how they're "connected." Things like this got handled among ourselves, and that's how it was settled.

So that was a hell of a weekend visit.

The other thing about being at Pitt is that I wanted to live like a campus star, but my family could only pull together $100 a month to send me, so it was up to me to make the most of it. I came up with two solutions. First, I made some good connections to buy bootlegged, name-brand "swag" and set up a buddy selling it in the student union. This was my friend Crazy Mike, who I have known since I was a kid in Kenilworth. Mike is a guy who always has some interesting stuff to give you. His car is kind of like a grocery store on wheels. He finds a lot of stuff that falls off trucks. Anyway, back when I was at Pitt, Crazy Mike came up to visit me and stayed for a while because he was able to hook us up with some good stuff. Mike needed a place to stay for a while, and I had this weird roommate at the time. He was a burnout, smoking marijuana all the time in the room. So I told this guy, "Look, I can't have you smoking dope around me when I'm on the team, and I have my friend Mike who needs a place to stay, so you have to get out." The guy looked at me and said, "What are you talking about? I'm not going anywhere." We were up on the twentieth floor or something like that, so I grabbed his big TV and tossed it out the window. It was one of those old TVs with the tube in it, so it made this really loud sound when it landed. Then I looked at him and said, "You're next." Crazy Mike had a place to stay. It was great, he got to the point where I got him a student ID and everything. He started going to classes, even though he wasn't really a student. Not only going, but he was participating. He's a character.

Anyway, this was back when all the Gucci stuff was really hot, like the sweatshirts and everything. So I would get the stuff, get it to my guy, and I would end up making like $3 a sweatshirt after it was all done. Crazy Mike was selling the stuff like, well, crazy.

Second, I hustled pool in bars around town and managed to turn that $20 into about $200 each month. I shot nine-ball, and I practically lived in the pool halls. I had a little hustler schtick going: I'd get a couple guys thinking I wasn't any good and then, *boom,* I'd take their money and their sticks. It wasn't a bad gig, but it was a grind. I was in survival mode, so we had to hustle.

My parents did the best they could, but there was only so much they could do. It's like when they dropped me off to go to college. My mother and father took me to the airport with my duffle bag full of clothes and other shit. My father gave me $50, dropped me at some airline, I think it was like People Express, shook my hand, and said, "Hey, man, good luck. Go get 'em." The plane ride was like three and a half hours because we got delayed for some reason. I get to school and it's like, *Okay, here we go.* Now I have to do my own laundry. All this stuff I've never done before. On Sundays I would go out for dinner looking for macaroni and there was nothing. I had to eat stew. It seems like a lot of little, stupid things, but it's like you're really making decisions now and taking care of yourself. You don't realize as a kid all the stuff your parents just take care of. It's very, very easy to make the wrong decisions, especially in college. You make a real wrong decision, you're screwed. It affects the rest of your life.

All the while, life is good during my first year. When I was playing football in high school, I didn't even know I was going to play college ball. But I get to college and I'm playing my ass off and everything is great.

One day during my freshman year, I get a knock at the door. I answer and it's Bill Chango, my Pop Warner coach from back in Kenilworth. He's flown all the way there, out of the blue. He looks at me and says, "Do you remember?" I say, "Yeah, I know why you're here." I remember what he had said—that I should find something else to do, that football wasn't going to work out for me. Well, he apologizes to me right then and there. Hey, he was rough on me when I was little, but he was classy. I respect that. Frankly, he may have been wrong, but it might have been the best thing to tell me because it lit that fire for me. When I made it to the NFL, he apologized again. When I won the Super Bowl, he did it again. Really, in some way, I probably owe him. It's not always about positive reinforcement.

As for Pitt, our team wasn't so good when I got there. The program was at the end of its heyday. They had Dan Marino at quarterback in the early 1980s. He was a Pittsburgh kid, grew up literally three blocks from campus. When he was a junior, they almost won the national championship, and they had a bunch of other great players like Rickey Jackson, Hugh Green, Jimbo Covert, and Bill Fralic about that same time. Unfortunately, Fazio couldn't really get us going. We lost five games my freshman season, which was his fourth season in charge, and they fired him. What sucked is that they blamed him for the program going downhill, and it was all BS.

What was worse is that they brought in this guy Mike Gottfried. I had no clue who this guy was. He didn't talk to us like men and find out what was going on. He just lectured us. I couldn't stand that crap. Then, he's wasting our time on stupid crap. Like he brings in the school fight song for the first practice. We don't even go on the field; we just sit in the locker room reading this page on the fight song. Seriously, he has us all in there and passes out pieces of paper with the words to "Hail to Pitt."

Until that point, I just thought it was some slogan on the side of Penn Hall. Now, I got nothing against good tradition. You need that stuff, but I'm not playing football to learn some song. I have to kick ass on the guy across from me, and I need a coach who is going to help me do that. I don't need to be singing, "Hail to Pitt, hail to Pitt every loyal son! Hail to Pitt, hail to Pitt 'til the victory is won!" Really, nobody sings the song unless we are winning or scoring. I had a feeling right from the start that Gottfried was a phony, and I turned out to be right.

Of course, being the loudmouth jackass that I am, I raise my hand and say, "Coach, what are we doing here?" Gottfried says, "Well, we're going to learn the school song." I say, "Listen, if I wanted to learn the school song, I would have gone to Notre Dame or Penn State or one of those rah-rah places. I'm here to kick somebody's ass, a hard-nosed so-and-so." That's me, Mr. First Impression. We went at it the whole time I was there. For that one, he made me run the whole stadium. Pitt Stadium, which was on campus, used to be one hundred steps up; it was one big bowl. I had to run up and down every stadium step. It was me and this other guy, Dave DiTamaso from Staten Island; we had to run all the steps. I ran every stadium step singing "Satisfaction" by the Rolling Stones. Gottfried thought he was going to break us, but it wasn't going to happen. He had no clue who he was dealing with. I was never going to quit.

Gottfried just hated that I wouldn't quit, and he did everything to try to throw me out of school the whole time he was there, right up to my senior season. What a prick. I blow out both my knees playing for that school, and he wants to throw me out.

That gets me to my first big hurdle at Pitt. After my sophomore season in 1986, when I have seventy-eight tackles, people are starting to talk about me like I'm pretty good. We get to the first part of the 1987 season, and I'm keeping it up, but then we play Boston College in the fifth game of the season, and Eddie Toner, a running back from BC, rolls up on my right knee. I tear the anterior cruciate ligament, medial collateral ligament, and lateral collateral ligament. This is pretty ironic because Toner and I became teammates at Indianapolis years later and real good friends. He wasn't trying to hurt me; he just fell into my knee. Anyway, of all the damage, the ACL is the big one, of course. The team doctor at Pitt was (and still is) this orthopedic surgeon, Dr. Fred Fu. He actually goes by Freddie, which makes his name sound funnier than it already is. Throw in the fact that he's originally from Hong Kong and speaks with a pretty thick accent and it's a little absurd, especially when you put me in the same room with him. I mean, could you have two people who are more different? But let me tell you, I was damn lucky to have Fu there to fix me up.

Of course, I didn't know this at the time, so I'm trying to figure out if Fu is any good. I'm like, "I want to come into a surgery with you, because I don't know if you're any good. I want to make sure you know what you're doing." I go in, and he does like nine surgeries in half an hour. This guy is unbelievable, and you should see the amount of respect he has from everybody. I come to find out he's one of the leading innovators in ACL repairs in the country. He's come up with this wild stuff over the years, like this thing called the "double bundle" procedure. Don't ask me, it's all way over my head. The important thing for me is that I totally trust him, and he's a good guy. We became very close—closer than I wanted, because he ended up fixing both my knees by the time I was done at Pitt.

On this first one, Dr. Fu takes a piece of tendon from a cadaver to fix the ACL. Beautiful, I got a piece of a dead guy inside me. The cadaver tendon fixes up my knee pretty good, and I'm ready to practice by the following spring. It's April 1988, and I'm on the practice field when *boom*, my left knee blows up. This time, it's the ACL by itself, but the thing gets shredded like a piece of crabmeat. Fu tells me there are a couple of ways to handle this one. The repair is going to be a lot harder, so one of his suggestions is to not repair this one at all. Just take the ACL out and work on the muscles around my knee and throughout my leg to make them really strong and keep my leg stable. If I do this, I'll have to miss the whole season by using a redshirt year. Okay, what the hell do I know? So I do it.

It turns out to be one of the best moves I ever made, because that's when I really got to know Buddy Morris for the next step—or should I say about four billion steps—in my journey. Morris was the strength and conditioning coach at Pitt. Crazy Buddy is like the mad scientist of conditioning. He's not only intense (he renamed the Pitt weight room "the Pitt Iron Works"), but he is like a freaking encyclopedia of information about training and nutrition and all the illegal shit that people are doing and why that crap is so bad for you. The Pitt Iron Works is so respected that it was named one of the ten toughest gyms in the country by *Muscle and Fitness* magazine. Morris is no joke; people from all over the country pay him serious props. He put me through some of the most rigorous stuff he had for like a year. You know that old stair-climbing machine with the perpetual steps that keep coming and coming? He'd put me on that for hours. I would do like two hundred, three hundred, four hundred flights of stairs on that machine. I was like crying because it was torture. He used to strap weights to my feet, then strap my leg to a pole and make me do leg curls. Seriously, this fucker killed me. But I played twelve years in the NFL, and it's because of Dr. Fu and Morris.

Morris built my legs up so strong that I didn't need an ACL. My hamstring and other soft tissue worked so well that they stabilized my knee. Up until that point, things had kind of come easily for me from a physical perspective. The real problem for me along the way was turning my mind loose and just doing whatever it was, overcoming the negative crap

I ran into along the way, and convincing myself to do whatever it was I had to do. This challenge was different. This was coming back from an injury, and not just coming back, but changing my body in the process. Morris pushed me so hard, and that really was the closest I ever came to quitting something. I've never quit a thing in my life, but that was close. And as much as that was a physical issue, it helped mentally too. It prepared me for what it was going to take later on, no question. He would break me down and break me down physically to the point where I wanted to quit and just go home and do some real-world job. But right as he got to that point, he'd start building me up again. I don't want to compare what football players do to what soldiers do, to going to war, but in football you do have to push yourself physically and sacrifice your body in a lot of ways. It's not war; nobody is dying. This is just for fun. But to be great, you have to get pretty damn close to that edge.

The pain was unreal at times. There were times I wanted to kick Morris's ass, I wanted to kill him. Oh, the times I wished I had a freaking bat. That's because I had never busted my ass like that. He was taking me to a whole different level. I got to the point where my hamstrings were almost as strong as my quads. But this is what I had to do to have a shot at my dreams. If I wanted to play football again, if I wanted a shot at the NFL, this was what I had to do. You have to know Buddy. He went to Pitt too. He was on the track and field team when he went there. He's the kind of guy who lives for what he does. He's not looking for a bunch of credit. You say to him, "Hey, Buddy, I really want to thank you for what you did," and he'll snap back, "Oh, go fuck yourself." He's all about toughness. He doesn't want to hear any of that cuddly stuff.

You have no idea what Morris means to so many guys who went to Pitt. He's not just a great trainer and a teacher, he's one of us. He's family. At one point, one of his daughters was dealing with cancer, and he called a few of us to come for a charity golf tournament in Sharon, Pennsylvania, this little town right near the Ohio-Pennsylvania border. Literally, there's like nothing there, but all of a sudden you have this huge group of great players like Marino, Fralic, and Chris Doleman showing up for this big weekend. It was a blast for all of us, and we'd all do it again if Morris asked.

One of the things the school did while we were there was raise the admission standards for the football team, and Gottfried started whining about that crap. It was ridiculous. Just coach: do your job and get good players. He was always worried about some crap, and the guys he hired, a lot of those guys were pricks too.

But besides all that, Pitt was perfect for me. The great thing for me about playing at Pitt was that if I could make it at that program, I was going to make it anywhere. In some ways, I'm not sure I would have fit in at Notre Dame or Penn State, one of those more straightlaced places. We may not have been that great by Pitt standards when I was there, but we still had tough guys. Our center part of the time I was there was Mark Stepnoski, who eventually went on to play for those great Dallas teams in the 1990s. It was a fight every day with Stepnoski.

Of course, there were some fights I got blamed for that I had nothing to do with. In fact, the closest I ever got to going to jail was for a fight I didn't even get into. This freaking thing even went to trial.

One night I'm out walking around with Burt Grossman, a defensive end who played with me at Pitt and who also would play in the NFL, and this fight breaks out. I've just had knee surgery, so I'm not about to get into any fights. I'm worried about getting healthy. After Burt and I stop to watch the fight, another guy we play with at Pitt gets involved. Our teammate clocks this other guy, and eventually the whole thing breaks up. Well, the kids who started the fight would claim that Grossman and I were in the fight and beat them up. Someone in their group got hurt, so they were trying to get us in trouble so they could maybe get some money out of us. It was total crap. It sucked because Grossman is such a good dude. He's kind of a loudmouth like me, but he also really cares about people. Years later, after his career was over, he won the NFL Teacher of the Year Award in 2011 for his work at Hoover High in San Diego. He does great work with at-risk kids. Even back then, it was totally against his nature to just beat up some kids for no reason.

Anyway, a day or so after the fight I go back to New Jersey, where I get a call saying that I'm being charged with aggravated assault. I'm told to come back to Pitt and go to the police. This is ridiculous. After all the times I actually kicked somebody's ass, now I get popped for something I had nothing to do with? This is crazy, and that's why I'm so pissed off. Finally, after like two years, we end up going to trial. After all this time, the derelict kid who tried to accuse me has joined the military, so he comes into the court in his dress uniform and everything. I'm thinking, *This jury is going to hang us, we have a soldier testifying against us.* Anyway, this guy testifies that I kicked him with my right leg when I beat him up. Except, I'm left-footed and I'd just had surgery, so there's no way I could have kicked him. The jury comes back with their verdict: "Not guilty."

Man, think about that irony. It was my bad knees that kept me out of one fight that could have really cost me.

04

MY DAD

In the early morning of July 10, 1989, my perspective on life changed. That was the day my father died.

I remember so many exact details of that morning and the day leading up to it. The day before, I'm in the middle of planning how to get back together with my girlfriend Kathy, who is now my wife. We've been broken up for about a year, and I'm getting her a gift for her birthday. There's a party for her, and I want to get her something really nice. So my father, my mother, and I go out to get her a gift. I want to do something really meaningful because I'm starting to figure out she's really the right one for me, so that's why I take my parents. I'm putting some effort into it. After we do that, my father and I go out for lunch, and we have a beer together for the first time. We're at a bar, just hanging out, and it's cool. It's like one of those stages of growing up, a rite-of-passage kind of thing. When I think back to that moment, I can't stop thinking about how my dad was passing on a lot of responsibility to me and somehow knew it.

He keeps saying these things like, "You take care of your brothers," "You take care of your mother." I'm twenty-two at the time, and all I'm thinking about is playing football and getting back together with my girl. All of a sudden, my dad is talking about some serious stuff with me, and I don't quite understand where he's coming from. It's weird. Sometimes I look back on it and think, *Was he telling me that I had to become the man of house?* I didn't understand it at the time. The sad part is, I was forced to understand it pretty fast.

The rest of the day goes on, and we're having a great time. We have about twenty-five people come by the house for a little backyard party. We're drinking some beer, having some hot dogs, it's all beautiful. We go to bed at around three in the morning. Within a few minutes, me and my brothers wake up to my mother screaming that my dad has had a heart attack. It's crazy. I'm performing CPR on him the whole time, trying to keep him alive while the ambulance is on the way. I am just working and working to keep him alive, it's all that keeps me from freaking out at that moment. He gets taken to the hospital, and we're following right behind. We get there, and one of my cousins who's a doctor at the hospital comes out and tells us my dad didn't make it.

Of course, my dad wasn't in the greatest shape at the time. He had already had a heart attack once before, in 1982. I was too young to really get what was going on with him, and he was okay after that. He rested for a few months, which drove him crazy, but he was back to being himself pretty quick. As I said before, he was probably five-foot-nine or five-foot-ten, about three hundred pounds. He was a real thick-built guy, always dressed to the nines. He used to say, "There's a lot of surface on a big guy. Make sure there are no stains on your shirt and you're always dressed nice." He was old-school.

By trade, my dad was a tool-and-die maker. He could fix anything and build just about anything. For me and my brothers, he was a real inspiration that way. Especially my brother Elio, who is a contractor now, and also the spitting image of my father. Elio used to follow my dad around when he was young. He probably spent a lot more time with my dad than me or my older brother Pete because we were already out of the house for a few years, so my dad and Elio were the last guys together most of the time. Elio actually does a lot of stuff at my house, fixing things like the ceiling in my kitchen, stuff like that.

When we were little kids, my parents opened a restaurant, a pizzeria, in Middletown, New Jersey. Man, running a restaurant is a tough business, and my dad had a lot of pride in that. He and my mom talked about how clean he used to keep it. That was important to him. The place had to be spotless, immaculate. They'd bleach it down at the end of every night. The other thing he did was make the workers open the boxes with all the vegetables outside before they brought the stuff into the place. He didn't want any bugs getting in there. To this day, I kind of believe in that same thing. When I had a condo in Indianapolis that I was renting from a teammate, we had a lot of fun, but the place never got trashed or out of control. You respect your property and somebody else's property. It's like I tell all these goofball young guys who make it to the NFL. They all want to buy cars and toys and crap like that. Well, buy a house or some property and take care of it. Buy something that appreciates in value, not depreciates.

My dad and mom helped teach us that, especially my dad with his work ethic and his pride. Eventually, he and my mom sold the pizza place, and he was going to open another one, but that's when he had the first heart attack, which was a real shock because he was barely forty years old. All of a sudden, he had to spend all the money he made on the pizza place on his health, on paying the bills and paying the mortgage. He was running his own place, he didn't have disability insurance and all that stuff. It was a real setback, and it upset him a lot. It hurt him to not be able to take care of his family the way he thought he should. He eventually went back to work for a place called Consolidated Fencing, driving the cement mixer out to the site and operating it. He was a Teamster, and on the side he was working with tractor-trailers. He also drove a limousine on weekends.

My dad busted his ass. He was up all sorts of hours between working and dealing with us. We'd get home late; he'd make us some food. It was constantly crazy around our house, and he was right in the middle of it all the time. He lived big. He was in a band growing up and even kept playing until Elio was born and there just wasn't any time left. Singing and playing in the band (even though he never had a music lesson in his life) was how he met my mom, and she still talks about what a great voice he had. He had this big personality to go with everything else. Even though he was a tough guy, he had a sentimental side. When each of us was born, he planted an evergreen tree next to the driveway. The funny part is that each of the trees grew to be about the same size as each of us, or at least relative to one another.

When we were growing up, I thought my dad was like clairvoyant or something. When our friends would walk in the house and my dad was sitting at the kitchen table, his back would always be to the front door, but he'd call out the name of whoever came in. He'd say, "Hey, Mike," or, "Phil, how are you?" Never even moved his head. How the hell did he do that? I thought he had eyes in the back of his head. He'd never explain it. It was like his little secret. Well, we figured out later that when the sliding glass door was closed, he could see the reflection on one side because the light was just right.

We'd watch the New York Giants every Sunday. My dad was a humongous Giants fan, and Sunday would be a big party during football season. My mom would cook five pounds of macaroni and would come in and out, watching the game. I didn't even know who some of these people were sometimes. I'd look at my mom and say, "Who the hell is this guy?" Maybe it was some guy off the street. Who knew? But everybody would sit around and watch the game, and my dad would walk in and sort of ask, "Who is a Giants fan here? Everyone raise their hand!" It wasn't really a question, it was a command. If you didn't raise your hand, you had to leave. He'd throw you out of the house. So even if you weren't a Giants fan before you came in the house, you were a Giants fan once you came through the door. Either that or you'd get thrown out of the house. My dad didn't believe in any other team. I remember back when the Giants were in their heyday with Bill Parcells and they were going to the Super Bowl a lot, my dad made one really over-the-top purchase. The Giants were about to play in the Super Bowl, and my old man bought a huge television—one of those early big-screen things. Of course, this wasn't some flat-screen thing. It was huge. That was the one time he really spent a lot of money on something. It's just too bad he never knew that I made it to the NFL or that I played the biggest game of my career against the Giants in the Super Bowl. That was probably the one day he would have asked, "Who's a Giants fan?" and kicked out anybody who raised their hand.

Two things hit me the most when he died: First, you have to be responsible. Second, you have to live big. Obviously, I felt a huge amount of pressure after my dad died. Even though I had my older brother Pete, I felt like I had to be the man of the house in a lot of ways. I was the biggest one of us, and I obviously had some opportunity with football, so I had to do something with that. This was right after I had missed the previous season with a knee injury and having to go through rehabilitation, so there was a lot of pressure to get out on the field and really prove something to everybody. I felt like I had to do something to support the family.

The second realization was almost as important to me. My father died at forty-eight years old. That's it. He had forty-eight years, and what I realized at that moment was, "Look, you don't ever know when you're going to die." That's when my life really changed. Now I live every day like it's my last day, and I never say, "Oh, I wish I could have done this," or, "I should have done that." People think I'm nuts because I think that life is completely backwards. I think you should go and live your life from the day you are born until you are about sixty. Then, at sixty, you probably feel like shit and you can't do anything—you should work from sixty until you die. So you should retire when you are young and work when you're older because you can't do anything. People work, they save all their money to do everything, then they turn sixty. You can't buy Wave-Runners when you're sixty because you can't even get on them. Your back hurts, your ass hurts, you've got hemorrhoids. It's completely reversed, I think. If you think about it, you know I'm right.

My dad lived like that in some ways. He was a fun guy who loved life, but he struggled to support a family. He had to work hard for a dollar. That's one of the reasons why, when I see a guy driving a cab or a limo, I give those guys extra respect because I know how hard a job it is. My dad was able to be really good at that because he had a very simple approach to handling people. He always used to tell me and my brothers, "Kill them with kindness." He'd have people going on and on, flipping out in front of him about something or other, and he'd say, "You know what? You're absolutely right." It would almost be that he knew how to turn people's switches off. He would just say, "No matter how much of a dick somebody might be, turn it around on them, and treat them like they're a prince." Trust me, that hasn't always been easy for me, particularly in my line of work. The NFL is not exactly a polite place, especially in the trenches.

In places where I'm not paid to beat the crap out of somebody else the way I am in the NFL, my dad's motto has helped me a lot. Yeah, I've had my fair share of brawls over the years, but there have been plenty of times when I knew that wasn't going to work. When you get into the business world and things get tense, you can't just haul off and beat the crap out of somebody, even if you really want to or even if they really deserve it. Even in an NFL locker room, it can't always be about fighting each other. Yeah, you do get plenty of that, because you're talking about one of the most macho environments you're ever going to find, but even in an NFL locker room there are times when you're better off killing a guy with kindness than throwing down some punches.

My dad also built a real strong sense of unity between me and my brothers. He'd look at us and say, "Me and your mother, we love each other, but we're not blood. You three share the same blood and you need to stick together." Other times he would say to us, "I want three things from you boys. That you fear me, that you respect me, and that you love me, in that order." You think about stuff like that and what he's really trying to say. He had this old belt that he used to hang on the kitchen door. It was one of those braid belts that had started to come apart. It looked like a cat-o'-nine-tails, one of those really nasty whips. He never hit us with it, but if we were ever a little out of control, he'd just look at that thing a certain way and we'd straighten up.

The other thing my dad was big on was dedication. He wouldn't ever let any of us quit something. It was like with Pop Warner football. By about fifth or sixth grade, I was too big to play in the games. Whatever the height and weight requirements were, I blew right past those in a hurry. But my dad kept me on the team even though the only thing I could do was practice. My practices were like games. By the time I got to high school, I had so much pent-up aggression from having to sit out that it was like releasing a caged animal. I was so ready to hit somebody for real in a game situation. Even when I was in seventh and eighth grade, I wanted to play so bad. We had this station wagon for a while. When we went to games, I wanted to play so bad, I would get in the back of the station wagon and start just doing push-up after push-up, trying to lose weight. I'd roll up the windows to keep the heat in so that I'd start to really sweat. People would come over and see me exhausted and say, "What the hell are you doing?" I'd just wear myself out trying to play.

As frustrated as I used to get, my dad kept me playing football. That's one of the reasons I never gave up whenever one of these challenges came up. Whether it was not getting drafted by the NFL, or blowing out both my knees and having to miss a whole season at one point in college, or even just dealing with his death at such a crucial time of my life, what my dad taught me has stuck with me my whole life. He had fight, that push to get something accomplished, and he passed it down to me.

Right after he died, this was mostly about responsibility. My dad was dead, and my mom was a wreck, of course. My brothers were trying to take care of her, and somebody had to start telling the extended family. This is not something you just start calling people about. You have to tell people straight up to their face that someone in their family is gone. I had to go to my grandmother's house and tell her that her son was dead. I had to tell my aunt that her brother was dead. That was rough. I wanted to be there to help them through it, but I also wanted to get home to my family. My grandmother knew it as soon as she got to the door. Probably because there was no other reason she was going to see me at 5:30 A.M., but probably also because she could see it in my face.

There were about 5,000 people who showed up at his funeral. It was unreal; all these people would come up and say how much my dad had helped them at some point or another. He was the type of guy who would be driving and see somebody stuck on the side of the road and stop and help them. I heard all these kinds of stories from people.

After we buried him, I had to think about what to do. It was July, and I had to get back to Pitt pretty soon to start the season. Was I going to go back? Did I need to get a job? All this shit was going through my head. One day, I was still just a kid. Yeah, I might have been twenty-two, but you don't know shit about life when you're twenty-two and you're in college. You don't know a lot about paying bills or having to take care of somebody else in your life. I went from being that young and dumb to the next day being a father figure to my two brothers. Trying to keep everything held together, not from home, but from college. So I'd come back from college all the time and go see my brother Elio whenever I could. He was growing real fast and was on his way to college. He had just finished his senior year and had played on a state championship team in football. Immediately after my dad died, Elio started talking about how he wasn't going to go to college; that wasn't such a good idea, but we were all pretty emotional. The good thing is, Elio went off to college, and then got his master's in education. He was a teacher for a while before he became a contractor.

My family was great. My mother and my brothers told me to get back to school and get moving. After all, we were all thinking that I was going to be in the NFL pretty soon once I played again. Nobody knew how hard it was going to be just to get a shot in the league. This was a time when

I could have used my dad the most: to help me get through all the crap I was about to deal with.

I was just coming back from blowing out my second knee and working my ass off. When I got back to college, my defensive line coach, that prick Frank D'Alonzo, was treating me like shit. D'Alonzo was the worst coach I had ever been around. He thought he was going to be tough on me, like he was supposed to be my dad or something. I had had my own father, and no one else was going to take his place. He was jerking me around like he was going to teach me some lesson. He kept telling me who I should and shouldn't hang out with. Even in the Pitt football media guide, he always had these backhanded remarks about how I had great promise if only I showed more maturity. We ended up getting in a pretty good fight, with me telling him, "Dude, my father passed away, you're not my father." After that, he tried to badmouth me with all the other players and the coaches. He was telling everybody, even NFL people, "Shit, Siragusa can't play." I found that out later. But as I was playing for him, I was always just thinking in the back of my head, *Okay, I have to be on a mission.*

Of course, you know what happened with the draft after my senior season, and how I almost never got a chance in the NFL. All those lessons my dad taught me about toughing it out really worked. Of course, the other lesson I learned was about people who stick it out with you. People who are loyal, like my wife. After about five years in the NFL, I knew I had to settle down and start the next chapter in my life. I also knew there was only one choice for me. I knew Kathy was the right woman for me because she was just like my family: loyal and mentally strong. She was the most stable thing in my life, behind me the whole way.

So about five years after I'd gotten to the NFL, maybe six years after my dad died, I came home and told Kathy I wanted to go down to the Shore. As we drove down the Garden State Parkway, I told her I wanted to stop at the cemetery to see my dad. When we pulled up at the gravesite and I got out of the car, I started to shake. As we got to the headstone, my eyes filled with tears, and I told Kathy I had something I needed to tell her. As I was talking to her, I couldn't get the words out because I was crying, and she had this really scared look on her face. She told me later, she thought I was about to break up with her. She couldn't have been more wrong. I had gone out and bought a diamond for her, and that day, right there in the cemetery, I asked her to marry me. She started crying and said yes. She was so happy and emotional, and I just thought, *This is pretty cool.*

My life's next big moment had taken place right there in front of my dad.

0|5

ROOKIE CAMP

Let's get back to 1990. I'm undrafted and looking for a shot, which is why I ended up signing with the Indianapolis Colts. I just looked at the roster, talked to a couple of people, and figured, this is where I have my best shot. There wasn't a lot more thought put into it than that. The problem was, they didn't think much of me either. Back then, most rookies get to come in for off-season workouts. I asked to do that, but the Colts didn't even want me to come in until just before training camp. Finally, when I got there, everything came together for me to start my career.

That's because, once again, I was told I didn't have much of a chance. This time, it was the Colts team doctor. Dr. K. Donald Shelbourne was this dude's name. I got examined by this guy when they first brought me to town. He looked at the one knee that I had the ACL reconstruction on and didn't have a big problem with that. But then he looked at the other knee, the one that has no ACL, and said: "Yep, no ACL there. Listen, son, you can have a good career, play maybe one or two, perhaps three years in the league. Good luck, I'll see you soon." This guy really pissed me off! Remember, I've been working with guys like Dr. Fred Fu and Buddy Morris, guys who have been telling me I can make it without the ACL if I do the right things, guys who have been with me for years, getting to know me and my body.

This guy Shelbourne looks at me for all of about twenty minutes and comes to the conclusion I've got two, maybe three years to play. Thanks, doc, that's just what I needed to hear, another jerk-off who wants to write me off. I remember when I was back for my sixth year, I saw him and said, "Shit, doc, I might outlast your ass." Truth is, Shelbourne is a good doctor and has a good reputation and all that, but he didn't really know me. He's just looking at a knee and saying, "This doesn't look right." There have been a handful of guys who made it in the NFL without an ACL or with a damaged one. Thurman Thomas and Garrison Hearst had ACL problems when they first got in the league, but just look at what Thomas did.

With me, having somebody else doubt me was perfect. Here was exactly the reason why I had to go through that miserable freaking weekend with my family and friends. Nobody in the NFL thought I was going to last, and here was the proof staring me straight between the eyes. Okay, I got it. I'll just tuck that one in the back of my mind.

So I go to rookie camp, which is a few days before the veterans show up. It's great, I'm busting my ass. Anything they tell me to do, I go a hundred miles per hour. I don't care what it is, seven-on-seven drills, goal-line, a light jog, I'm tackling somebody. They think I'm nuts, and I don't give a damn. I'm making this team. We do about three days of that, and then the veterans show up. No matter what I did in those three days, nothing could prepare me for what I was about to see. I'll never forget this: I'm sitting on the side, and we are just getting done with practice, and I'm exhausted. I see this big, long, white Mercedes pull up. I'm thinking to myself, *Is this the owner?* I've never seen a Mercedes this big. It has windshield wipers on the headlights.

It's pimped out with the tinted windows and the whole deal. The door opens up, and there is a light-skinned black dude with red hair who gets out. I'm thinking, *Who the hell is this guy?* It's Fredd Young, this four-time Pro Bowl linebacker. He's got diamonds everywhere: earrings, sunglasses, the whole thing like you'd see in the movies. After he gets out, he opens the back door of the car, and two poodles come out, both with diamond-studded necklaces and a leash. This freaking guy is either so full of it or he's the baddest mother who ever played the game. I say to myself, *Holy crap,* and watch while the press comes running over to him. He's all cool with his Texas drawl (he's from Dallas) and says, "Hey, how's everybody doin'?" I'm thinking to myself, *What the hell is this?* I'm thinking, *I have to get my crap together, this stuff is serious.*

If that weren't enough of an introduction to the NFL, the topper was the tag team of running back Eric Dickerson and coach Ron Meyer. Now, we're talking about one big-time trip. These guys were special, joined at the hip in terms of both success and controversy. Back in the late 1970s, Dickerson was *the* big-time stud running back in the state of Texas, and Meyer was coaching at Southern Methodist University. That was back when SMU was part of the old Southwest Conference with Texas, TCU, Texas A&M, Arkansas, and all those programs. The conference was supposedly out of control with cheating. There was cash and cars and women and all sorts of stuff happening. It wasn't much different than a lot of other places in the country—it was just over the top, from everything I've ever heard. It was like everything in Texas, where it's all about being big and bold. Evidently, they were brazen about it.

Anyway, Dickerson was the real deal in high school. Shit, he was a Hall of Famer in the NFL, so you can only imagine what he was like in high school. Supposedly, he was going to attend Texas A&M but ended up going to SMU at the last second to play for Meyer. Now, Dickerson is slick. He's never said anything about what he got, and I can respect that. But Meyer, this guy was something else. "Slick"—and not the good kind—is only the beginning of how to describe Ron Meyer. This dude was forty-nine years old when I got to Indy, and he would wear this *Top Gun* hat, no shirt, and these ball-hugger pants hiked way up above his shorts all the time. This guy had like a mammal toe thing going all the time. And the hair—Meyer had the best hair in football this side of Jimmy Johnson.

So Dickerson went to SMU to play for Meyer. They ended up with this awesome team. They won the Southwest Conference title in 1981, but were already on probation for some recruiting violations, so they couldn't compete for a national championship. They were known as "the Pony Express" because they also had Craig James in the backfield with Dickerson. James wasn't nearly as good as Dickerson, but he was still a really great player. He played in the old USFL and then moved to the NFL, where he gained over 1,000 yards one season with New England and helped them get to a Super Bowl. The upshot of all this is that Meyer's program was cheating way back then and got busted in a serious way. SMU ended up getting the "Death Penalty," which basically destroyed the whole program. Not surprisingly, Slick Meyer got out before the whole thing got out of control. He ended up leaving in 1982 and taking a job as head coach with the New England Patriots. Give him credit: he did a nice job the first year, getting the Patriots to the playoffs during the strike season. He even made history in that first year in the NFL. In typical Meyer fashion, it was by bending the rules.

On December 12, 1982, the Patriots were hosting Miami at old Fox-boro Stadium. That place was a freaking dump. The stadium had Astro-turf at the time, and it was snowing like crazy—one of those games where as soon as you get done shoveling the snow from the yard lines and the sidelines, you have to do it again. Neither team could move the ball very much, and the game was scoreless going into the fourth quarter. Finally, New England got in range for the go-ahead field goal with 4:45 remaining in the game. Now, the footing was brutal because of the snow. For the kickers, it was really easy to slip as they were turning to kick. So Meyer got the bright idea of having the guy running the snowplow on the field clear a spot for the kicker. Now, there was no real rule for this, but it was totally taking advantage of the situation. On the other side of the field, Dolphins coach Don Shula was furious. Having played against Shula, I can tell you, the man knows how to do furious.

So they cleared the spot for the field goal, and kicker John Smith hit a thirty-three-yarder for a 3–0 win. Shula refused to shake hands with Meyer and protested the game, which would be dubbed the "Snowplow Game," but NFL commissioner Pete Rozelle couldn't do anything because there was no rule against it. Rozelle totally agreed with Shula, but his hands were tied. The best part of the whole thing is that the guy driving the snowplow had just got out of prison on work release. His name was Mark Henderson. A few years later, they asked Henderson about it, and he said, "What are they gonna do, throw me in jail?" I liked that answer.

Back to Slick Meyer. After that, things in New England went down-hill pretty good. In 1984 he was fired in the middle of the season, despite having a 5–3 record, because the players hated him so much. Think about that: you're winning and your guys can't stand you? That's Captain Bligh/Doug Neidermeyer–type stuff. Worse, the Patriots went on to the Super Bowl the next year, and Meyer wasn't around to get any of the credit.

At the end of the 1986 season, Meyer got hired by Indianapolis. The Colts were 0–13 at the time, and Meyer immediately led them to three wins, so they thought he was some kind of freaking miracle worker. The next season, Meyer pulled another one of his over-the-top stunts. Of course, it had to involve Dickerson. The 1987 season was marred by another NFL strike. The league played two games, the players went on strike, the league brought in replacements for three games, and then the players slowly started to come back. During all of this, Dickerson was complaining about his contract again with the Rams. Now, understand that Dickerson was one of these guys who could basically name his price and still be worth it when he was in his prime. The dude gained more than 1,800 yards in three of his first four seasons, including an NFL-record 2,105 in 1984. The dude was ridiculous, particularly for a guy that tall. An amazing north-south runner, he'd make one cut and be gone.

So on Halloween 1987, Meyer decided he had to have Dickerson again. But Meyer didn't just trade for him. He traded the house, the car, and the vacation home. It ended up with three teams and ten players involved. Among other things, the Rams got three first-round draft picks and Buffalo got Cornelius Bennett. In the short term, the deal worked because the Colts won the AFC East that year. It was another quick turnaround for Meyer, so he got all this goodwill built up, even if they didn't have a draft pick until the third round in 1988.

The bigger problem was that the Colts got a guy who was on the downside. Dickerson was still great: in nine games with the Colts in 1987, he still rushed for more than 1,000 yards, and he'd have more than 1,600 in 1988 and more than 1,300 in 1989. But by the time I got to Indy in 1990, Dickerson was just about done, and Meyer knew it. So what did Meyer do in 1990? It was time for another big, splashy move, so he traded four players and two first-round picks to get quarterback Jeff George. When they were scouting him, George just wowed them with his arm. Meyer once said George threw so hard it was "like throwing it through a car wash and the ball not getting wet." Whatever, too bad Meyer didn't scout George's personality. Years later, Meyer said, "I just didn't see the competitiveness" with George. Like I said before, scouting football players is way more than just figuring out who can throw or run.

All the while, Meyer was still in love with Dickerson, even though Dickerson was holding out for a new contract, causing all sorts of problems, and eventually got suspended for four weeks. Here's a classic moment: The veterans all report, and suddenly I see Dickerson for the first time, and I'm like, *Shit, it's Eric Dickerson.* We're all getting ready to go to practice with the veterans there. Again, I'm all jacked up and ready to practice, trying to make this team, thinking about who I'm going to hit. This is going to be like the first practice we had with all the players in front of the fans. So we have fans showing up and players making their way to the field, stretching, throwing the ball around a little.

So Dickerson is running for a pass, just jogging lightly really, and he slips just a little bit. His foot moves like maybe four inches, and you can hear him say, "Oooh." It's not like he's in pain, just a little sound like something is uncomfortable. All of a sudden, here comes Meyer in the *Top Gun* hat and the ball-hugger yeast-infection pants. You'd think it was somebody dying or something. Meyer starts screaming, "Practice is over, it's canceled," and he runs over to where Dickerson is standing. Dickerson isn't even limping. He's just walking around, he maybe felt a little twinge or something, and here comes Meyer, freaking out and canceling practice. They signal to have a cart brought over, and I'm just looking at this thinking, *What the hell did I just get myself into?* I'm thinking that they're going to call 911 and have a life flight helicopter take Dickerson to the hospital. This is how serious Meyer is acting. One guy feels a twinge, and we have to cancel practice. This is nuts.

So we all have to go back inside after the practice. Now, it's a real pain in the ass, because not only do you have to go back inside after not getting a chance to take out some aggression by hitting somebody, but you have to take tape off after you haven't had a chance to sweat. Getting a sweat going makes the adhesive come off. So we get back in the locker room, and they have Dickerson on a training table in there. He's lying there, and there are like ten doctors in there surrounding him. I think they drove doctors in from other cities just to see him. I'm thinking, *Oh my God, this guy must really be hurt.* The other thing I realize is, I'm not hitting him or Jeff George anytime during camp or I know Meyer is going to cut me. Everybody else, I'm good. Those two, they're completely off-limits.

Now, understand that the locker room we had in training camp back then was basically a high school gym with lockers set up inside. The next day we come in, and they have completely moved the lockers around, pushed everybody out of the way like none of the rest of us matter. The whole team depends on whether Dickerson is healthy or not. This is what Meyer is setting up. So they move us all out of the way, and there are six guys in blue scrubs standing around, and they bring in a laser machine the size of a small house that they're going to use to penetrate the little pull in Dickerson's hamstring.

It was crazy, but Dickerson's health determined everything for us. It determined Meyer's mood, whether we practiced, had meetings, the whole deal. If Dickerson had a toothache, it would be like the end of the world to Meyer.

This is how crazy the NFL was when I got there. The coach and everybody else were worried about all the wrong shit. Instead of getting the team ready, we were waiting on one guy. What happened if that one guy got hurt? The world ended. We had veteran guys who were more concerned about whether the rookies got chicken for the flight home from a road game than whether we actually won the game. Speaking of food, my first year with the Colts they would give us bag lunches with like peanut butter and jelly sandwiches. You have guys you're paying hundreds of thousands of dollars and you're giving them peanut butter and jelly? Seriously, my high school team was more organized than that.

The point is, this is what I was dealing with. I got this nutty head coach who liked to show off his nut sack while kissing the asses of his star players. This dude didn't know who I was and frankly didn't really care. Fine, whatever, it probably worked to my advantage in some ways. And when you're a rookie, it should probably be that way anyway. You should have to earn some respect.

On top of that, we had Dickerson, who was cocky as hell. Another time in camp Meyer comes in and yells, "All right, let's do a walk-through." That's where you practice at basically walking speed, maybe a light jog at most. You're just trying to get it in your head what you're supposed to do. This time Meyer has these tight Sansabelt slacks on, the mammal toe going full bore, with blue sunglasses and no shirt. What the fuck is this? I mean, I like things to be loose, but this guy looks like he's ready to go to a club, not run a practice. Whatever, we head out for the walk-through. As usual, I'm fully taped up and ready, I even have my football cleats on. I just want to kill somebody so I can prove I belong. Meanwhile, Young and Dickerson come to practice riding bikes and wearing flip-flops. Seriously, bicycles. Worse, they park them right on the 50-yard line, and we do the walk-through at the 45. That just makes me more pissed off. I'm desperately trying to make it, and these guys don't give a shit.

Of course, this was all part of the learning process. Not that Young and Dickerson were right, but it's a little different when you've been in the league for a few years. Walk-throughs are walk-throughs. You don't want to waste your energy in a walk-through. You want to learn. You ain't making the team at a walk-through. But when I was a rookie, I didn't know what was going on. People were flying around, it was fast as hell, and I was just trying to keep up. All I knew was I was a rookie, and all I was thinking was, *If they put me in, I'm killing that quarterback. I don't give a damn if he has the ball or doesn't have the ball. I'm killing him.*

I remember one game that season when I got a fifteen-yard penalty for roughing the quarterback. I didn't give a damn. That's the mentality you have to have as a rookie. You can't be out there thinking so much. You're going off raw testosterone, just plain balls. When you're a rookie, you really don't understand the concept of what's going on. They have all these terms like "over," "under," and "firehouse." The coach is talking in the meeting room, throwing out these terms, and I'm looking around and thinking to myself, *Is everybody getting this?* No. The guys who stop and try to decipher everything, they're screwed. The guys who make it are the guys who say, "To hell with all that crap, I'm going to go rip them up." It's really that easy. You've got to just go out there, get recognized, and let the coaches know that you're going to go and kill somebody. You worry about learning who you really have to kill later on.

One of the other strange stories from that season was that the NFL had just recently started testing for steroids. Since I wasn't on steroids, I wasn't very popular with some of the veterans who obviously were juicing. Now remember, the 1970s and the 1980s were out of control when it came to steroids. Completely out of control. Just look up stories on guys like Tony Mandarich and Steve Courson and you'll get an idea of how big steroids were back in the day. When I got in the league, guys were still doing it big-time, and you could tell. It was easy to figure out. You'd see guys who just didn't have the frame to carry that kind of weight. There were guys on every team who you knew were normally maybe 240 pounds, but they were carrying 290 or 300.

So one day I come into the locker room, and there's this one guy on the team who is going from guy to guy, and he's having these little hush-hush conversations. Finally, he comes up to me and asks me, "So, are you clean?" I don't know what the fuck he's talking about, so I say, "Yeah, I just showered. I used Irish Spring." He gives me this look like I'm an idiot, and I say, "What are you talking about?" So he asks me if I'm taking steroids. I'm like, "Dude, I'm trying to lose weight. What do you think?" So he asks me to go piss in a cup for him, put the cap on, and take it to him. Now, at the time, the FBI agents would come in and actually watch you piss, so I'm thinking, *How is he going to use it?* So he tells me he's going to go piss everything out of his bladder, then catheterize my piss back into his bladder and piss that out. I'm like, "You're going to what? Dude, why are you doing that? That's disgusting!"

He looks at me and says, "Do you know how hard it is to make the kind of money we make in the real world?" It's amazing what some guys will do for money. After that, I was really happy when the NFL commissioner back then put in testing for everybody, and then the union would park a trailer out front and take a second specimen just to double-check everything in case there was a screwed-up test. But all that stuff during the steroids era was just crazy. So many guys were freaking out about whether they were going to be able to play.

Most of the other stuff was pretty normal. The rookies had to wash the veterans' cars, which sucked but wasn't the worst thing in the world. We had to go out after practice, when I was exhausted and just wanted to rest. Look, you have to pay your dues. That's part of it, and that's how I grew up. It's like starting in business. You're supposed to start in the mail room and work your way up. These days, so many of these rookies think they just have it made. It's a joke. You ask some rookies to do kickoff team or punt team, and they think that's beneath them. They figure 'cause they never had to do it before they don't have to do it now. Well, dumbass, who's supposed to play special teams in the pros if you don't do it?

When I got to the Colts, anything they asked us to do, I raised my hand. I'm in, I'll do it. They said, "Okay, we're going to do a kickoff team, can anybody kick off?" I'll kick off. I told them I used to kick in high school. Give me my shoe; I'll be the backup kicker. "Can anybody punt?" I can punt. Of course, that's not how those jobs work, but when one of the coaches asks, "Can anybody long-snap on punts?" I raise my hand. He says, "Okay, come to the meeting tomorrow morning, you're going to be the long-snapper."

Well, I realize at that moment that I don't really know how to long-snap on punts or kicks. But my brother Pete knows how to do it. I've got an 11:00 A.M. practice the next day, and I have one night to learn how to long-snap. That night, I jump out the window of the dorm room, and I sneak out to a pay phone. This was back before we had cell phones like we do now. I call Pete. I say, "Pete, listen, I need to learn how to long-snap." He says, "All right, I'll come out there." I say, "No, no, no, I need to know right freaking now, Pete. I got a ball with me, tell me how to freaking long-snap." I'm on a pay phone, and I'm right next to this school yard. He says, "Put your hand, the middle finger down the seam, grab it like you are going to throw it, and don't look back. Make sure your forearm is smack against your thighs when you go back." I'm like, "All right, hold on." So I go and walk off fifteen yards, and I'm looking down, and I throw it and it's wobbling a little bit. I go back and say, "It's wobbling." He says, "Turn your wrist more." He's talking me through it until one in the morning, like two hours. I'm snapping it until finally I get it down. The next day I go to practice, and the coach calls, "Punt team." I'm on the starting punt team, cool. I go out there and I'm throwing it back pretty good. I'm left-handed, so the spiral on the ball is a little bit different, but I'm getting it fucking back to the guy. After that, I practice long-snapping every night after the regular practice is over.

We went through the rest of training camp and the preseason. I think I had two sacks or whatever. We played against Jim McMahon at one point. He was with Philadelphia by that time. I got a chance to hit him, and the penalty flags started flying. I thought it was raining flags because I hit him late. Like I said, I don't give a shit; if I get near anybody I'm just going to kill them. People are going to know who I am.

So the last day comes—it's cut-down day. We come in, and there are tags on the lockers of the guys who got cut. I say to somebody, "Listen, if there's a tag on my locker, I'm going to go punch the head coach in the face. I'm going to do something, I don't give a shit." I go in, and there's no tag. I sit down and I say to myself, *Holy shit, I made this mother-freaking team.* Well, not twenty minutes go by, and a guy comes around and he goes, "Hey, Goose, grab your playbook, Coach wants to see you." So now I think, *Shit, he's going to cut me.*

I get my stuff, go in there, sit down, and Meyer doesn't pay attention to me. He looks around like I'm not even there and starts talking. "Well, son, you've got a long way to go to make an NFL team, and I look like the biggest jerk-off right now in the NFL." I'm thinking, *What's he trying to say?* "We run a five-man front." It was actually what most people know as a 3–4 defense, with three linemen and two outside linebackers close to the line. "Nobody in the NFL carries three noseguards. I got Harvey Armstrong, and I got Mitch Benson backing up who we drafted in the second round last year. And we've got you. But you are the only guy who can long-snap, so I gotta keep you. But you are a long way from playing in the NFL, and it doesn't mean you're going to be here tomorrow." I keep my mouth shut. I want to tell him to go fuck himself, but I keep my mouth shut. He gets done, and I go in the locker room, and I call my mother and tell her, "Holy crap, I made the NFL." She goes nuts, and everything's cool.

By around the middle of the season, we were playing a Monday night game at home against the New York Giants. Benson, who was starting by then, got hurt, and I got to go in. This was like a dream. The Giants are my hometown team. I was going to kill these guys, it was great. From that point, I never looked back. I was in the lineup the rest of my career until I retired. Benson? Out of the league after the 1991 season.

If you think the only thing that was crazy was the coach and the top players on the team, well, just understand that it all starts at the top. Back then, Bob Irsay was the owner of the team. This was the guy who had moved the Colts from Baltimore to Indianapolis in the middle of the night to avoid attention, so you know he was a real peach. He died in 1997, and his son Jim took over the team. That was just before I left the team for good, and I had one really interesting one-on-one experience with the elder Irsay a few years after my rookie season. But I got a taste of what he was all about my rookie year.

We got into the season, and we were losing games pretty bad from time to time. We'd be down fourteen points or something like that in the second half, and we'd have to throw the ball to get back in the game. That's just the way it goes. Well, that should be the way it goes on most teams. We'd be on the sideline, and the phone to the sideline would ring. One of the assistants would answer it and then walk over to Meyer. It's Irsay. He wants to let Meyer know, "Hey, I'm paying 29 [Dickerson] a lot of money, I want to see him run the ball." Run the ball? We're down fourteen, you can't run the ball. Well, Meyer starts nodding his head and saying, "Yes, sir," then hangs up the line and yells to the offensive coordinator, "Run Dickerson on a stretch play or something." Seriously? Are you kidding me? We're trying to win and the owner is bitching about how Dickerson isn't running the ball enough? Am I in the Twilight Zone? Compared to this, I had more structure when I played in high school. Thank you, Bob Taylor.

0|6

GUNS AND
LOSSES

et me put this in proper perspective: Indianapolis was a great place
to start my career. I couldn't have picked a place with better people
and more fun, as it turned out. I also got my start in the media business
with my own radio show there, and that was after we went 1–15 in my
second season. We also had some pretty cool moments. We went to the
AFC Championship Game in the 1995 season and made the playoffs the
next year. I got married while I was in Indianapolis. I partied and had a
good time. I met my good friend Eddie Toner, a guy who had busted up
my knee when he played at Boston College but ended up being a great
guy once we met in Indianapolis. I was coached by Ted Marchibroda,

who eventually got me to Baltimore. Those seven seasons in Indianapolis really set up my life for a lot of great things.

But, man, we had to go through a lot. Mostly, a lot of losing, a lot of bad football, and some really weird people along the way. I've already talked plenty about Slick Meyer and Eric Dickerson, and I'll tell you about Rick Venturi and Lindy Infante in a minute. But we had one guy who went way beyond that. In one afternoon, he topped everybody. He was in a gang. Or at least he had been in a gang growing up. That didn't bother me. I get it and get along with everybody.

Anyway, in the middle of that year, this guy comes up to me and Eddie Toner and says, "They're going to cut me today. When they cut me, make sure you guys stay near the complex, because I'm going out to my car and getting two nine-millimeter guns, and I'm firing about thirty rounds over the building. I'm going to try and hit one of those mothers because I don't like anybody on this team but you two. During stretch, stay near the building." I think to myself—but I make sure not to say it out loud—*No wonder you're getting cut. You're out of your freaking mind.* Doesn't this guy think that maybe this is a bad idea for his future, not to mention some of the coaches?

Of course, this guy is more than a little crazy. There were stories about him even before the day he got cut. He lived in this apartment building next to the Colts' practice facility where a bunch of players used to live back then. This guy lived on the second floor. One day the guy who lived on the floor below him came into the building and was really pissed off. Turns out, the night before, the guy who lived downstairs was sitting there watching TV when a bullet came down through the ceiling and shattered the glass table about three feet in front of where he was sitting watching the game. For whatever reason, the guy upstairs—the guy who is now threatening to shoot up some coaches and players because he's going to get cut—fired a shot through the floor and down through the other guy's apartment.

That wasn't the only time either. This guy used to be waiting in lines at like Burger King or McDonald's, and if there were too many cars, he would fire a shot or two into the air. After everybody scattered, he would just drive up and make his order. I'm serious. The other thing he'd do is that at lunchtime, he'd take the plastic knives and forks and stick them in his socks for practice. If he didn't like somebody, he'd pull out one of the utensils as we were practicing a return coverage or something and he'd try stabbing and cutting the guy. Yeah, it was just plastic, but that shit hurt. Nuts, just nuts.

So ten minutes later, I see the guy walking out, and he says, "Remember what I said." *Holy shit, they cut him.* I'm on the way out to stretch before practice, and it's like, *What the hell do I do now?* After a while, me and Eddie Toner hear a couple of pops of a gun. I think this guy fired like fifteen rounds over the top of practice. As I said, it was lucky that no one was hurt, but it was totally nuts! Because the Colts' training complex was out in the middle of the woods, I think everyone just thought it was a hunter. Eddie and I knew better.

I was thinking, *How the hell did this crazy mother get a gun?* Well, as I came to find out, it was really easy to get a gun in Indiana back then. In New Jersey, you had a lot of hoops to get through to get a gun. In Indiana, guys were buying all sorts of guns. They would come in the locker room with Uzis, handguns of all kinds. I had an AK-47 in my locker at one point. Like I said, it was really easy to get a gun in Indiana back then. I had never fired a gun until I got to college, and we never had one around the house when I was growing up, so it's not like I was all gun-crazy. It was really just something fun to do after I got to the NFL. You could walk into Don's Guns, and they would literally give you any gun you wanted to go test out. I mean anything, fully automatic stuff, Uzis, the whole bit. All you had to do was have an Indiana driver's license and you could buy a gun. Hell, back then there were times it was even easier than that. The guy who ran the place—Don, I guess—used to come to our practices at training camp in Anderson, which is about thirty miles outside of Indianapolis. He would just show up, open his trunk, and have a bunch of guns in there for guys to buy. If you wanted to buy one, all you had to do was give him cash, and he'd write out a receipt, easy as that. To think about it now, it's incredible. It was really just a way to blow off some steam. You'd get a gun and a bunch of ammo, go shoot at a target, kind of just blow some shit up.

It was like the whole team had an arsenal. It was ridiculous. This one year, they said there was going to be some ban on certain types of gun, so a bunch of the guys went out and bought like a truckload of these guns, thinking either they weren't going to be available or the price would go way up after the ban took effect. I guess you could say there was gun speculating. It was unreal.

Anyway, so all my friends from Jersey would come out, and we'd go shooting. Me and my friends would go in, throw down a few hundred bucks, and say, "Hey, give us one of those and one of those," and then go shoot all this ammo we bought. We'd go to these gun ranges, and Eddie Toner, my roommate, was always saying, "Tony, look at these crazy people." There would be people walking into the range, yelling about how their gun wasn't working. It would be loaded and they'd be pointing the guns everywhere. Toner was always worried that somebody was going to do something stupid. He was probably right, but what the hell? We were having a good time. Then all the guys on the team found out, and they started buying guns like crazy. Every day there would be some player walking in saying, "Hey, look at this fifty-caliber I just picked up," or, "Look at this assault rifle." It was really the wild, wild West. That was Indiana back then.

We even had guys who would go hunting and come to practice straight from the woods or wherever they were. I remember Tony Bennett, a defensive end who played next to me, would come in still dressed from being out there. He'd have camouflage clothes on, the camouflage stuff on his face, the whole bit. He'd walk right into a meeting looking like that. He'd put his shotgun or rifle right in his locker, and he was ready to work. We were like, "Dude, what have you been doing?" It'd be like eight or nine in the morning and he'd be looking like this. He'd tell us that he went out at 4:00 A.M. to start hunting. If you didn't know better, you could walk into one of our meetings and think he was the leader of one of those antigovernment military groups and we were the followers. Today there's no way this could ever happen, even on a football team with all these aggressive guys. People would be freaking out if they heard there were guns all over an NFL facility.

Now, I'm not exactly Mr. Hunter like Bennett or those guys. But I have a pretty great story about my first big hunt. We had this offensive lineman on our team named Ron Solt in 1992. He had played for the Colts a couple of years before I got there. He was a first-round pick in 1984 and was actually one of the guys the Colts got as part of the John Elway trade. Anyway, he made the Pro Bowl one year as a guard with the Colts, went to play for Philadelphia for a few years, and then came back to the Colts in 1992. Solt was friends with a relative of Toner's, so Solt was kind of looking after Toner, who by this time was rooming with me at the condo I was renting out.

It turns out that Solt was this big hunter, and he owned a big spread of land just north of Indianapolis. So he invited us up there one day to go bird hunting. We all get there, and Solt has this stuff down pat. It's like the

GI Joe Commando Raid edition with the camouflage and everything. I mean, he's like Mr. Outdoorsman. Seriously, it's almost intimidating. I've got on a tank-top T-shirt and some of those Zubaz pants. Remember, I'm from New Jersey. About the only hunting we do is the kind that features a police helicopter zooming along with the getaway car down the turnpike. Anyway, Solt also has this friend with him, a guy who's a war veteran. I think he served in Vietnam. I also have my cousin Danny with me— I should probably mention here that I always have someone with me. My wife says she thinks I need an audience, that I can never be alone.

Anyway, Solt is going over all these rules and shit, and I'm thinking, *When do we start shooting?* I have my adult ADD going, and I don't want to hear all this stuff. Eventually we split up and flank this area where the birds are supposed to be. Solt and Toner go over to the other side of this big hunting area, the veteran guy goes to this third spot, and so Danny and I are together on one side. I send Danny back to the car for our guns and some ammo. I wait a couple of minutes to let Toner and Solt get to wherever they're going, and now it's time to shoot.

I have my automatic weapon, and I figure I have to get these birds moving—you know, get them out of the woods. So I fire a few rounds. Now we have birds flying, and it's great. I start firing, *bap, bap, bap, bap, bap.* I'm firing at anything that moves and is white. I know it's not Solt or Toner because they're in their camouflage stuff, plus they're not flying up in the air. I stop for a minute and see a bunch more birds off in the distance and fire in their direction. We're having a great time. Every time I run out of ammo, I have Danny right there with more for me to reload with. This is a great time.

Next thing I know, here comes Solt, and he's a little salty. He's a gentleman about it, but I can tell he's seriously peeved. It's like I've somehow upset the hunting universe. Of course, I did do a couple things wrong.

First, I shot right over the top of where he and Toner were standing. That wasn't so smooth. Then he tells me that some of the birds I shot at were sitting on a power line. Fortunately, I didn't shoot down the line, so that's all good.

Then Solt tells me that this veteran guy he brought along started freaking out like he was back in 'Nam, like he's got post-traumatic stress syndrome or flashbacks or something. Solt says he had to go calm the guy down and talk him out of his hiding place or something like that. How am I supposed to know that firing an AK-47 was going to do that to this guy? Solt is all pissed about that too, that I'm using a gun like that. You're not supposed to hunt with an automatic weapon or a semiautomatic weapon? What's that all about? You have a bunch of birds you're trying to shoot. What's the best way to do that? Fire a bunch of bullets. Of course, Toner is laughing at me like he always does, telling everybody that I was shooting at anything that moved, like butterflies. Whatever, dude. Then Solt sees all the ammo shells scattered around where we're standing, and he's flipping out again. Calm down, dude, I'll clean it up. I tell Danny right then to pick up all the shells. Solt never invites us back.

Anyway, we actually did play some football while I was in Indy. My first year, we opened up 0–3. We played the Bills, who turned out to be pretty good (that was the first of four consecutive seasons in which they went to the Super Bowl), we almost beat New England, and we lost to a pretty good Houston Oilers team with Warren Moon. I wasn't playing a lot just yet. Early in my career, they actually used me most of the time as a third-down pass-rusher. Most people wouldn't know that was what I did early in my career. By the time I got to Baltimore (actually, by about three or four years in the NFL), I had worked my way into being a run stuffer on first and second down. In fact, I had sixteen and a half sacks in my six years with the Colts. Not bad for some guy who most people thought couldn't move (or be moved). Of course, I might have had more sacks if I actually had a couple of moves. I was a straight bull rusher. For those not exactly down with football lingo, that means that you charge straight ahead like a bull with its head down. Now, most offensive linemen will tell you that it's a lot easier to stop a guy with only one move. Let me tell you, I had one move for twelve years, and I made it work pretty damn well.

In our fourth game, we finally got a win. Shockingly, to me, we beat Philadelphia, the other team that offered me a contract after I went undrafted, the team loaded with so many stars. That was pretty cool. Plus, we beat them on the road, so I had a lot of family around. We won the next game against Kansas City for two in a row, but we were streaky the whole season. We'd lose three, win two, lose two, win three. We finally finished 7–9. Not great, but it was a start. You figure we had Jeff George at quarterback and things would get better, no problem.

The problem was that, as all this was going on, Dickerson was on the decline, and as I said before, this guy had been brought in by Meyer to be the centerpiece of the team. When I was a rookie, he only started eight games and played in eleven games total. For the first time in this dude's career, he gained less than 1,200 yards in a season. Dickerson opened his career with seven straight 1,200-yard seasons. That's crazy. Before I got to the NFL, this guy was a total thoroughbred, a true elite athlete.

The problem was, he knew it too. He was a different type of guy, that's all I can say. He was always creating waves, causing some drama. Great player, but he was a strange dude. One time a bunch of us went out to his house in Los Angeles. He had a black Lamborghini and a white Lamborghini, exact same model. He had a black Mercedes-Benz and a white Mercedes-Benz, same model. Just a different kind of guy.

A lot of other guys were different, just not as into themselves. We had

Donnell Thompson, a defensive end who played next to me. He used to sit in the locker room drinking black coffee and smoking Parliament cigarettes. He had one of those big, tall ashtrays right next to his locker. We'd come in at half, and Thompson and a bunch of other guys were having big cups of coffee. Think about how nuts that was, especially compared to these days, when guys are measuring their purified vitamin elixir in eyedroppers. Hell, even back then I just wanted an orange or something light. Black coffee in the middle of the game is pretty hard-core. Thompson would be sitting in his chair, swigging coffee, taking a drag of a Parliament, and saying stuff like, "Let's run this blitz." I loved it. He was a player, all man.

Our second year, things didn't go so hot. Well, that's an understatement. We went 1–15, and it was worse than that because we went 1–15 and couldn't score for shit. Our defense was okay, or at least it seemed that way. Sometimes it's hard to tell when the other team doesn't have to try. I know what you're thinking. This is the NFL; everybody has to try to win games. Trust me when I tell you, the teams that played against us that year didn't have to try most of the time. We had eleven games when we scored seven points or less. We had five where we either got shut out or scored three points. I mean, we were awful on offense. Look, I'm a team guy, and I don't like to point fingers. You win and lose as a team. But sometimes you're so bad on one side that it just is what it is. We scored 143 points in 16 games. That's nine points a game.

Now, if there's a silver lining to all this, it's that having gone through that, I had an easier time dealing with our title year in Baltimore in 2000. That year, everybody made a big deal when we lost three straight games after scoring six points or less. Are you kidding me? That was nothing like what I saw in 1991. The other thing that happened for me was that, with the team playing so bad, the media in Indianapolis was desperate for anything to talk about. Just something entertaining, anything. Enter yours truly: Tony Siragusa, the radio sensation of Indianapolis.

I knew I wanted to do a radio show, so I approached this rock station in town. But they gave us like the worst time slot of the week, the time right before the Monday night game at one of the local bars. We're on location with all these fans around, but it's not like we can really talk about football. I mean, we sucked. The fans didn't want to talk about that crap. So I started talking about anything. It became like a variety show. You want to know about how to clean your car, I'm your guy. You want to know about sex, I'm the original Dr. Drew. Whatever you want to talk about. Still, we were struggling to get listeners. Then Toner became part of the show. Not that anybody knew it. We didn't have anybody calling in to the show because nobody knew who I was and nobody wanted to talk about football. So Toner went into the next room and started calling in and asking all these off-the-wall questions. He'd ask stuff like, "I just wanted to know, because I have really bad gas, does anybody on the team fart a lot in the locker room?" Or he'd ask me questions about how to handle his taxes, or what I thought about the stock market, or maybe where to take a girl out on a nice date. Toner, who's a seriously brilliant guy with a twisted sense of humor, would make up all these voices to make it sound like we had all these callers, and I'd make up whatever I could off the top of my head. It was crazy, just great. Suddenly, people were listening because listening to this show was like watching a car wreck.

Of course, Toner found a way to get himself in the show. He used to call pretty regularly, like he was some fan, and say, "Why doesn't Toner play more?" and I'd play along and say, "Oh yeah, we gotta get Toner on the field." Or he would start asking questions about the games and all the stupid things the coaches did, totally second-guessing the coaches and the front office. I'd just let him rant on and then say, "Well, that's your opinion," not really defending the coaches or the front office, but not getting myself in trouble. The other thing he'd do, just to mess around, was say, "This is Tom from North Dakota," or, "This is Jed from Des Moines." This was in the days before streaming radio, so that was impossible. Then I'd bust his balls a little bit. I'd start talking about Toner's dating life. I'd say, "Girls, don't get involved with Toner, he has a very small package of skills, if you know what I mean." Or I'd talk about how he used a thimble for a cup. Or I'd say Toner went on a date the other night and it was such a disaster the girl got up from dinner and just left, or whatever came up. Toner would get pissed at me, but I'd just do it even more. If I know I've got you, I keep on going.

Anyway, the show started to catch on. By the second half of the season, the bar where we did the show was mobbed every Monday night. By the end of the season, the station was talking about bringing me back the next year. This was awesome. Eventually, the station moved the show from Monday nights to Friday morning because it was such a draw. Even though Friday was a light practice day every week, the Friday morning time slot was a little tough because we'd go out after the long practice on Thursday and party all night. So we'd have the limo basically take us straight to the station on Friday morning.

Then there was this one year I held out, in 1994. I told the hosts of the show, these guys Bob and Todd, that I wanted to be on air every single day, and they were more than happy with that. The Colts were hating it because I basically had my own platform to present my side of the whole thing. I was just killing the Colts, talking about how they missed having a good defensive tackle. Later on, Toner became my producer, and he used to mess with me all the time. When they asked me football questions, sometimes I didn't know all the players. I'm not some stat geek who studies all the players. I know the game and how it's played. Who everybody is? Whatever. But they'd ask me a question sometimes, and I might not know who the slot receiver for Seattle was, so Toner would whisper in my ear, "Bobby Brady is having a great year," or, "Don Knotts is just awesome." Of course, he's just making it up. I had no idea those were TV characters, so I'd say it, and he would just bust out laughing at me later.

Toner and I had some great times. He's such a good dude. We ended up rooming together for three or four years. When I first got there, I was renting out Duane Bickett's condo. Bickett was a linebacker with the Colts, and he had this extra place he had bought early on. The place had a hot tub in the garage. Nice. Now, I kept the place in really nice shape and never trashed it—except that I didn't clean the hot tub regularly. One year Toner and I got back to Indy, and we hadn't been there in a while. So we decided to get in the hot tub to relax a little. It was dark in the garage, so we weren't really noticing anything. I submerged my head a few times. Afterward, we both got deathly ill. I was puking for days. I hired somebody just to sit next to my bed in case they had to rush me to the hospital. We come to find out the water was this greenish-black color. It was disgusting. It made me ill just to look at the water again.

Another time when we were living at the condo, I had just purchased this new paintball gun. I hired this guy to go out in the backyard and be the moving target. Now, I gave the guy a helmet and a trash bag to wear, but it probably got a little out of hand after I hit him for like the thousandth time. I think the guy ended up cowering behind the barbecue. We'd have poker games at the place all the time, or we'd go out. Toner was such a pussy sometimes. He'd start complaining about how he needed his beauty sleep or whatever. He'd start saying, "You know, I'm not Eric Dickerson and Marshall Faulk all rolled up into one. I gotta get some rest if I'm going to be able to play." Rest? You're an athlete. I'd get back from practice, nap for an hour or two, and I was good. He didn't work that way.

After a couple of years of that, we moved into this new house in this nice development in the suburbs. It was this area of town where they were turning old cornfields into subdivisions, so we could get this place for a pretty good price. Of course, we moved in and, this being Indianapolis, everybody in the neighborhood was very friendly. We had people bringing over fresh-baked cookies, brownies, and casseroles while we were moving in. Of course, two single football players weren't exactly the perfect new additions to the neighborhood. We must have been quite the sight. We would drive up on our Harleys, making all this noise. Or we'd start fighting and wrestling around, and that would get out of control. I'd start grabbing Toner, and he'd try to fight me off with like a frying pan. We would end up in the front yard, Toner waving a frying pan at me as the neighbors walked up to us with a plate of food or something like that. What a sight we must have been.

We had some great times at that house. One time I looked at Toner and said, "We need a pet." Toner was, as always, looking at me like I was crazy, but I was serious. We needed a pet. Not just some big dog or something, but something exotic, something wild and aggressive. So we got this big lizard. I think it was like a Komodo dragon. Okay, not a Komodo dragon, but something like that. Well, at the store, the lizard was really easygoing, you know, kind of friendly for a big lizard. They must have had that thing doped up on lizard tranquilizers or something. We got the thing home, and it started to get wild, really aggressive. The other thing was, this lizard was like a meat-eater. It wasn't looking for plants; it wanted steak or the next best thing—which could have been us. Eventually, the thing was just getting out of control. It was climbing all over the place and hissing at me and Toner like we were going to be its next meal. We finally got this thing into one of the bathrooms and locked it in there. I didn't know what to do with it, but I would throw some food in there.

Of course, the thing had to take a crap, and the really awful part is that the air vents in this house were on the floor. So the lizard was crapping and pissing right into the vent or something like that because the house started to just smell awful. Finally, we were trying to figure out a way to get the thing back to the pet store. I wanted my money back, but I would have given it back to them for free. Before we could get it in my truck, the lizard got loose again in the garage, so we locked it in there. You could hear this thing knocking stuff around. It was angry at us for the whole bathroom incident. I can't really tell you what finally happened because the PETA people would probably have my ass, but the lizard didn't make it.

Toner and I had a blast. We went to the last Super Bowl at the Rose Bowl before the Rams and the Raiders moved out of town. Buffalo played Dallas in that game. Anyway, one of the events the week before the game was this "Super Bowl of Golf" with all these quarterbacks and other people who were participating. We got there, and of course, we wanted to play. But we were there in like cutoff jean shorts and T-shirts, and all these quarterbacks were dressed to the nines in their hoity-toity golf outfits. We did a bunch of stupid stuff, like we entered the "Super Bowl of Sumo Wrestling." I was going to wrestle, and Toner got all dressed up in this pimp outfit to act like he was my manager. Fortunately, that got canceled.

This one year in Indy, I bought a truck with a snowplow on the front. Don't ask me why, but I thought it was a good idea. Really good, as a matter of fact. Normally, it doesn't really snow that hard in Indianapolis, so it's not like they have this big snowplow business. But this one year, it snowed like crazy. So I ask Toner, who is from Boston, "Hey, you know how to use a snowplow, right?" He says, "Sure, Tony, I got it." So there's all this snow on the ground, and we go driving around. We're in this one neighborhood, and people see us and they're asking, "Can you plow my driveway?" I'm saying, "Sure, for $200." No problem. I say $300—no problem. This is great, we're going to make a little money here, it's all good. I'm going to be Mr. Plow (just like from *The Simpsons*, thank you very much FOX-TV).

As we're doing this, a few people recognize me, and they're yelling out my name and all this stuff. This is great. I'm going to be Tony "Mr. Plow" Siragusa. So we get to this one really nice house where they're having a party. It's nighttime, and everybody looks like they're having a good time. They're happy to pay us. The only problem is that Toner really doesn't know what he's doing. He's giving me all these excuses like, "It's not dropping right," whatever that means. I'm like, "You're from Boston, what's the problem?" He yells back at me, "Oh yeah, ya big dope, everybody from Boston is supposed to know how to use a snowplow?" Of course they are, what's this guy talking about?

Anyway, we're outside this nice house, and they have this combination circular driveway with a straight driveway next to it. So Toner starts backing up after picking up some snow, and all of a sudden he's off the circular driveway and the plow catches on a power line. I don't know, but we're pulling on it. Then the lights in the house go *poof.* All of them go out. Then out go the lights in the next house, and the next, and the next: *poof, poof, poof.* I look at Toner and just yell, "Get out of here!" If those people could, they'd probably still be chasing us.

We'd go down to Fort Lauderdale in the off-season and stay with one of my buddies, Joey Esposito. He had a house down there, and he was trying to make it as a cook in one of the restaurants. The plan was always to go down there, work out hard, and really watch what we ate. But somehow other stuff just got in the way. I don't know, it's South Florida. What do you want me to say? There were "distractions." Anyway, we'd be down there at Joey's house, and I'd invite a few people down. At first, it'd be me, Toner, and linebacker Matt Vanderbeek. Then a couple more guys would show up. Then a couple more. It was great. We'd all go to the beach and hang out during the day. The only problem we had was that Joey would go with us, and Joey is really hairy. He's got that man rug all over his chest and his back, so we had to help him clean that up. We couldn't be hanging with Sasquatch on the beach. So we went out and got some Nair For Men and sprayed that all over him. Of course, we didn't really read the instructions first. I think we left it on a little too long because Joey was like screaming in pain at one point.

But back to the 1991 season. We still sucked as a team, and that was brutal. When we dropped to 0–5 that year after a 31–3 loss to Seattle—that trip was so long that I thought we had gone to like Japan or something—Slick Meyer got fired. He wasn't going to be missed, but then they promoted Rick Venturi, who was our defensive coordinator. Well, he was sort of our defensive coordinator. I had been there for a year and a half, and I barely knew the guy. Really, I had barely any idea who this guy was. He took over and had this meeting right after Meyer got fired.

Venturi is kind of a little guy. He looks like he was maybe a safety or something, but he's not exactly a commanding presence. He's kind of a nervous-looking guy most of the time. Well, we're all sitting there, and he said, "All right, gentlemen, let me just tell you a little story." We're thinking to ourselves, *All right, let's see what he's got.*

He started rolling like he was hyped up on hallucinogens. "This week we're playing the Pittsburgh Steelers, and when we get to the stadium, it's like back in the days when the Vikings would get on their boat, and they sail and all the guys would come off, and the head guy from the Viking clan would go back and burn the ships. That's what we're going to do this week. We're going to burn the ships." I looked around and thought to myself, *Is this guy freaking crazy? What the hell is he talking about?* He kept talking about how "there's no turning back, we're going forward. All right, guys, break now for your meetings." I wasn't the only guy who thought he was nuts. The rest of the players were saying, "Holy shit, now we have this guy and he needs Prozac." We were 0–5 (we got to 0–9 before we finally won, thankfully against the Jets, so I got another win when I went home to the Jersey area), and this guy is talking about burning the freaking building down.

Fortunately, the Colts were smart enough to figure out that Venturi wasn't exactly built to be a head coach. That's when I met a guy who really helped get my career going in a good direction, both in Indianapolis and later in Baltimore.

GOOSE TALES WITH . . .
EDDIE TONER

Eddie Toner played three years in the NFL with the Indianapolis Colts. After rooming with Tony Siragusa for almost the entire time and going into business with him, Toner eventually moved to Florida, where he could be protected from his friend by "gates and alligators." He's kidding, we think.

"Yeah, we roomed together for three years, technically. Every so often, I would move out and stay away as long as I could. I would say I was going to the store to get groceries, and I would find an apartment. I would put all my stuff in my truck, and Tony wouldn't notice. A couple of days later, Tony would figure out I wasn't there and say, 'Hey, E, how come you're not at the place anymore?' I initially couldn't tell him the truth about why I was moving out because he'd object. I'd say: 'Tony, I have to get some sleep. I can't stay on this team and go 24/7 the way you do.' Eventually he'd find out where I was living by following me to my place. The next step was always a fight. I could hold my own until he started using his size and wrestling skills. As soon as that happened, the fight would end and eventually I would be back living with him. Our fights were usually a great source of entertainment for the neighbors since they mostly took place in our driveway or on the front lawn. The only time we probably crossed the line was when Tony bought a house out in Carmel. This was a brand-new house in a new development built on an open field. On moving day, me, Tony, and the movers were carrying boxes out of the trucks into the house when the new neighbors started bringing over trays of food to welcome us to the street. Tony thought this was great because it gave him an excuse to stop working.

He was sitting in a big chair in the driveway, eating from the trays of food, playing his best Eddie Haskell. Things got out of hand when it was time to get the twelve-person hot tub out of the moving truck and into the garage. This tub was bigger than a full-size car. He was barking instructions to us on how we should do it from the big chair, while eating the food, and that was it. Tony and I ended up on the front lawn fighting in front of the new neighbors. This fight lasted longer than the others because I had a box of kitchen stuff near me on the lawn. I hit him with anything I could get my hands on: pots, pans. We didn't see any neighbors for months after that.

"He'd been in Indianapolis a year or two before I got there. My first day in town, I signed my contract and went to shake hands with the general manager. I think the second sentence out of his mouth after saying, 'Congratulations, welcome to the Indianapolis Colts,' was 'Stay away from Siragusa.' I didn't think too much about it at the time, since I'd never met Tony before. One thing was obvious: he was making an impact with Colt management. He was being included in the Welcome to Indy kit.

"Anyway, that first day I went into the locker room and Tony came in late for his off-season workout. The trainer was yelling at him and pushing him out of the weight room because he went in there with no clothes on, buck naked. He came back to the locker room with a big smile. I later learned he had a boat trip or something planned that day. Great insider tip from the GM: stay away from the loud, crazy person.

"For the next four or five months, as we went through the off-season and then training camp, Tony didn't say a single word to me. I guess he figured why bother making friends if the guy might not be around that long. Then we get to the end of training camp, We're at Anderson University, this beautiful Christian school about an hour outside Indianapolis.

They tell us at the end of the last training camp practice, the guys who didn't have a place yet, they could go back and stay at the team hotel for a couple of days until the final cutdown. I'm headed for my truck, and here comes Tony, engines gunning in his Bronco as he drives over these telephone pole–style barricades they had in the parking lot. He's driving right at me. I'm thinking, *What did I do to him?* Maybe someone else I know is with him in the car. Tony drives up and says, 'Where you going?' I tell him I'm headed to the team hotel. He says, 'I got an empty spot; why don't you live with me? Follow me to my condo.'

"So I follow him, and he opens the door to this two-car garage, and the first thing I see is this hot tub with fake carpet all around it, fake palm trees, and mirrors everywhere. What the heck is this? The water is this murky green, like it hasn't been cleaned in months. It's all starting to flash back to me, the GM saying, 'Stay away from Goose.'

"We had a charity dinner that night for the Colts downtown that we had to be ready for. I'm the kind of guy, since I've always been the twelfth guy on an eleven-man roster, who needs to be there early, make sure I do everything right. The dinner is supposed to start at 7:00 P.M., and I'm dressed and ready to go at 5:00 P.M. I've got a sport coat on, and I'm waiting for Tony. Well, of course, he's working on his Harley. He's telling me to relax, and he's telling me I'm way overdressed. He's saying, 'This is the pros, you don't have to get dressed up like that.' I'm saying, 'Tony, you sure? The coach told us to wear a sport coat. He says, 'Listen, bro, you haven't been here. Trust me.'

"So I'm standing there watching him fix the Harley, and I start asking him all these questions. This is actually the first time we have a real conversation. I made the mistake of asking him 'Why is the water green?' Now it's like 6:30 P.M., and Tony says, 'Yeah, let's try and fix that,' and he starts draining the hot tub. I'm getting more and more nervous, and he says, 'Don't worry, bro, it's only ten minutes away. Trust me.'

"He then convinces me to not wear a sport coat. I have on a shirt with jeans and he's dressed in a Harley T-shirt with grease all up and down his arms because he couldn't get it all off. We leave at 7:00 P.M., and the event is supposed to start at 7:00 P.M. We get there, take the elevator up, and the elevator opens up right into the room with the light flashing right on us because the rest of the room is dark. Oh my God, everybody is dressed up, looking good, and they're all staring at us, the two guys who are late and look like hell. That's Tony, he puts you out on the ledge sometimes, but if you're one of his guys, his friend, he won't let you fall. Well, you may fall, but he'll do his best to catch you.

"There was the time he convinced me I needed to go ask for more money. I had been bouncing back and forth between the roster and the practice squad, and that's a big difference in money. So I'm getting ready to go sign another contract for the roster, and Tony tells me I need to ask for more money because of the 'mental anguish' I've been through, bouncing back and forth. I'm thinking, *Who am I to ask for more money?*

"I just want to sign the contract and go out to practice. Tony says, 'Bro, trust me, you have to ask for more. This is how it works; take advantage of the situation.' He's telling me 'You're a great negotiator, Eddie. You need to say that last night was really tough on your psyche.' All I'm thinking is I just want to go to practice. Tony is saying, 'Bro, you have to stand up for yourself.' He wouldn't let it go. I eventually get it in my head from Tony that I have the leverage to ask for more money, and I walk in there to sign the contract and ask the GM for like $10,000 more. The GM looks at me and says, 'Are you out of your mind? Get out of here!' I'm stunned. I just got released, I am now heading for the parking lot. Now what am I going to do? As I was getting into my car, the GM's secretary comes running out and gets me to come back in. The GM calmed down and was actually laughing, and they put the contract in front of me again. He said, 'Are you crazy or have you been hanging out with Siragusa too much?' I think they gave me like another $5,000. I don't even know. All I'm thinking is, *I need to sign these papers as fast as I can before the GM gets pissed again.*

"I go back in the locker room, and I'm stunned with what just happened. Here comes Tony, the big smile, and talking about how, 'See, you listened to the big guy, and what happened? Now you can go out and get a nice car.' He's yelling, 'I told ya, I told ya,' and then starts talking about how he deserves some of the action, like he was some great agent. For the rest of the year, he thought he was Jerry Maguire, giving everyone advice on how they should handle their contracts. He would say 'You saw what I did for Toner.'

"Tony has this little saying, 'When you're with me, you're with me and when I'm with you, you're still with me.' I've heard him say this many times in many different situations over the years. I think it's a perfect description of who he is. Tony is a true friend who can be counted on to stand by you in good times and bad. His heart is too big for his body and that's a big body."

07

ME AND TEDDY

After the whole Slick Meyer disaster was over, the Colts finally hired Ted Marchibroda. This moment was almost like at the end of *Animal House* when the kid says, "Thank you, God." Finally, we got a guy who was at least a little sane. I love Teddy: he's a total straight shooter and a guy who knows how to run a whole team.

Now, our offense still wasn't great, but it was better, and we had some serious optimism going. We had the top two picks in the draft, so we took defensive tackle Steve Emtman and Quentin Coryatt. As I told you before, neither of those guys ended up having a great career, but at least we thought we were going to get something big going, some momentum.

So after the first seven games, we were 4–3 and had this awesome game at Miami when Emtman intercepted Dan Marino at the end of the game and returned it ninety-five yards for a score. Pretty awesome play for a defensive tackle down in Miami in the humidity. What's too bad is that we lost four games after that, but then we won the final five games of the season to finish 9–7. It was the best year we had had since I got there.

The more important thing was that Marchibroda was changing the attitude. It wasn't long after Teddy got there that I became his guy in the locker room, and the other players knew it. Teddy was good to me. For instance, we came to an understanding about my weight. I was working on it, but I wasn't always going to make it. He didn't make a big deal out of it. The flip side was that I made sure the guys in the locker room did what we needed to do in practice and meetings. We were going to have a good time, but it wasn't going to be stupid.

Consequently, I sort of became the consigliere of the locker room, which leads me to one of the great all-time stories. One night a week, all the black guys on the team would go to this one club. I would tag along once in a while. So one night we're at this club. I'm the only white guy in the place. No problem; I'm fine, totally comfortable. One of my teammates—I'll call him Lenny, just for the sake of this story—is on the dance floor dancing with this blonde, who is the only white woman in the place. Again, no biggie, everybody is cool. The girl is dancing up a storm, doing "The Running Man" and all this shit, and she's definitely into Lenny. It's all good, and it turns out, as I find out the next day, that they go back to his apartment for a little after-party. Lenny was living in this apartment complex near the training facility where a lot of the young, single players lived. The place was this U-shaped building with a courtyard in the middle, so basically everybody could see everybody else going in and out of their apartments.

At the time, Lenny also had just bought this Rottweiler puppy. So he gets the woman home, and they play with the dog for a minute before the two of them make their way to the bedroom. Now, as they're getting down to business, the woman says, "Before we go any further, I have to tell you something." Lenny is like, "What's up?" Now remember, as he's telling me this the next day, I had just seen this chick the night before dancing away. She tells Lenny, "I have a fake leg." Lenny is dumbfounded for a second as she takes off her leg and shows him this stump. I was dumbfounded too, so I said, "What did you do?" That's when Lenny starts saying, "Well, you know, she needed her some Lenny."

"What about the stump?" I asked. Lenny said, "Oh man, that was like the strongest stump you could ever imagine." I'll let your imagination take it from there. I'd have been laughing, except Lenny was kind of freaked out at this point, asking me for a big favor.

So he and the blonde go at it for a while. Like he kept saying, she needed her some Lenny. As they're going at it, the dog jumps up on the bed a couple of times until Lenny finally takes him out of the bedroom and shuts the door. Then, when they wake up the next morning, they're getting dressed and the woman goes to get her leg, but she can't find it. It turns out the dog took it out of the room and was chewing on it the whole night, this expensive prosthetic leg. The toes are gone, the rest of it is gnawed on—it's a wreck. Now the woman is upset, and she expects Lenny to pay for a new leg. The thing is so chewed up, she can't even get it on. Lenny offers to give her a ride to the hospital where she got the leg, but she has to hop, and as he looks outside the apartment, he sees a bunch of guys from the team. He doesn't want them to know he's been banging a one-legged woman all night. So he tells her to stay in the apartment, and he goes down to the hospital. By now, he's running late for practice, but he's trying to take care of the woman. He gets to the hospital, and they tell him a new leg is $1,200. Now he's really freaking out.

Lenny finally gets to the training facility, and now he's late, so not only does he have to pay for the leg, but he's worried that he's going to get fined another $1,000 or so for being late. That's where I come in. Lenny is begging me to go to Teddy and ask that he not get fined. I'm standing there wanting to laugh my ass off, but I'm also like Judge Wapner, trying to figure out if Lenny has a case. Finally, I tell him, "Okay, I'll talk to Teddy." So I go to Teddy, and I'm like, "She was doing 'The Running Man,' but Lenny found out she only had one leg and the dog ate the leg and he went to the hospital to do the right thing. Seriously, she was doing 'The Running Man.'" Teddy keeps saying, "I don't want to know, I don't want to know." He's closing his eyes and throwing his hands up in the air like it's almost painful to listen. Finally I say, "Can you just cut him a break and not fine him?" So Teddy didn't fine him, and it worked out fine.

On the subject of black and white and any other issue that divides people, let me say this: none of that shit matters on a good team. You put that shit aside. But if you have problems in a locker room, you have to deal with it, and I was always an equal opportunity administrator. I guess you could say I was pretty unfiltered, which only works in a locker room. We had this one time when we had kind of a loudmouthed black guy on the Colts. He's in the locker room one day, talking really loud about how "the brothers, we have to stick together against the white man," and all this shit. Yeah, yeah, I get it, he isn't really talking about his teammates, but that's how it comes out to a lot of guys. It's the kind of shit that breaks up a team. So I'm sitting there and start shouting, "Hey, all you white guys, David Duke is having a rally next week, we all need to attend or make donations. We have to stick together, you know." Duke was the head of the Klan back then. Now look, no self-respecting Italian guy from New Jersey is giving a dime to the Klan, but I'm making a point. We're a team, not a bunch of black guys and a bunch of white guys. The black guy who's been talking starts saying, "Goose, come on, man." All the other guys, black and white, start laughing. That's the kind of stuff you have to take care of in the locker room.

I busted everybody's chops. We had this executive named Bob Terpening. He did all the contracts and stuff and worked closely with Bob Irsay, the owner. (I'll tell you a great story about him in a minute.) Anyway, Terpening was this fat guy who used to always sneak down on Fridays to grab food from the players' table. Friday was the day when rookies had to bring in food, so it was kind of a special day. Plus, I was always fighting like hell to make weight. I was starving myself and taking water pills to flush my system. (My buddy Eddie Toner used to rip me all the time for eating pasta on the nights before weigh-ins.) Anyway, I'm fucking starving, waiting for a weigh-in, and here comes that dickhead Terpening to steal our doughnuts. I get on the PA system in the building and start yelling, "You fat asshole, stop stealing our food." Man, I was mad about that.

Weigh-ins always sucked until I was able to reach a fair deal truce with Marchibroda. Teddy understood I was trying. I'd have some friends of mine from New Jersey with me, and we were always trying to figure out a way to rig the scale so that I made weight. We'd call one of the auto yards back home in Jersey, looking for a spring or something. Meanwhile, Toner was sitting there mocking me, that little jerk. "Oh yeah, this is the secret to being a pro," he'd say. "Water pills, making yourself throw up, and starvation. Everybody thinks you're drinking protein shakes with extra vitamin D and a glass of pickle juice to keep from dehydrating. Yeah, this is the way to prepare for a game in two days." He was such a dick sometimes, but he was pretty damn funny.

Marchibroda was old-school: he understood how tight the locker room had to be and that it had to come from the players working together on their own, working through whatever issue anyone might have with another guy. Then came the football part of it, which was important, but it was the football, not all the other crap.

For instance, weight training is fine, but it's not the be-all and end-all. We'd go into the weight room, and we'd have these guys get really serious, like they were working out for Mr. Olympia or something. Look, being strong is important in football. That's like one of those "no shit" statements. Really, you have to be strong in football? You don't say? But there's being football strong and being weight-room strong. I see it all the time. These guys want to get all muscled up and big, but that's not how you play football. You play football with leverage and burst. Yeah, you need power, but you need to be able to move to get that power.

I used to piss off all the big weight-lifter guys on the team. I'd come in, and some guy would be doing four or five hundred pounds on a dead lift, or the bench, or what have you. He'd have his little weight-lifter outfit and belt on. He'd wrap his hands and use chalk on his hands for a better grip—taking it all so seriously. Whatever the most that had been lifted, I'd look over and say, "Put ten more on that." Then I'd walk over and lift it like it was no big deal. I wouldn't warm up or anything—just snap it up and then walk out of the weight room. Those guys would be so angry at me because I was just mocking them.

Marchibroda brought some normalcy to the team, but there were still some wild times, and it started right at the top. One of the best stories is what I like to refer to as "the Christmas Party from Hell." Soon after Teddy took over, Irsay held a Christmas party at his "farm" just outside of town. I guess you call this thing a farm because it was this huge piece of property that had what they called a barn in the back, behind the house. This really wasn't a barn as much as it was like a big catering hall. He'd host big events back there, like a fund-raiser for the governor or whatever. You know, rich guy stuff. Anyway, this thing was mandatory, and all the players were pissed about it. It was the end of the season, and we weren't very good; most guys would have liked to just stay home and rest. But Irsay wanted his party, and he was going to get it.

At least, he was going to get it after I got there. Now, before we get to the highlights of this party, I have to tell you how we saved Toner's career that night. Just after I get there, I'm standing there talking to my teammate Duane Bickett. Toner is there, and he's brought his sister to the party because she happens to be in town. We're all talking, and Toner offers to go to the bar to get drinks for like six or seven of us. He gets the drinks and is bringing them back, but just as he turns Irsay walks right into him. Toner has this one drink with cranberry juice in it, and it spills all over Irsay's shirt. Now the old man is pissed. He's like yelling at Toner, "Who are you? What's your name?" Bickett and I see this right away and head over there. Bickett tells Irsay, "Oh, sorry, Mr. Irsay, this is my cousin so-and-so." I start backing him up, saying, "Yeah, yeah, that's Bickett's cousin." Irsay doesn't buy it at first and says, "Don't you play for me? What's your name?" We distract Irsay long enough for Toner to get away, find his sister, and then hide for a while until he can figure out how to escape. For the rest of the time Toner played for the Colts, he would find places to hide every time Irsay came around.

Back at the party, a little while after that, I walk over to this empty bar in another part of the place. The place is completely empty, and I'm thinking, *The alcohol is the same over here, right?* There's like three or four hundred people at this thing, and I'm really not in the mood to mingle. I'd figured I'd make an appearance, go see the coach to make sure he saw me, and then get out of there pretty quick. Well, as I'm standing there talking to the bartender and getting my drink, here comes Irsay. Now understand, Irsay was like seventy years old at this time. He's talking kind of loud as he walks up to me, like he's already pretty lit up. He starts saying, "I heard about you, I heard about you. I heard you can drink. Let me tell you, I'm the one who can drink." He's mumbling some other stuff, and I'm not saying much. I'm just trying to keep things calm. Then he looks at the bartender and says, "Get us two shots of Jack Daniel's." I say, "Okay, but just one shot, Bob. I drove my motorcycle and everything." He wants none of that. He just says again, "I heard you can drink. Well, let me tell you, I can drink." So he orders another shot and then another.

Now he's getting louder and louder with every shot and people are starting to gather around. There are media people around, and I'm trying to get the old man to stop. It's not that I can't drink with him, but he's getting sloppy, and I really do have to take my motorcycle back to my place. The last thing I need is a DUI after a Christmas party. But this is the owner, and I can't insult the guy at his own party at his house. As we get past shot number three or four, Irsay is just mumbling and Teddy comes over with his wife. Teddy is looking kind of nervous, and I'm looking at him like, *What the hell do I do?* Teddy's wife stands next to Irsay, and Irsay puts his arm in hers, in just a friendly way. Then Irsay starts to ramble about Teddy: about what a great coach he is, what a great man he is, and what a great wife he has, until all of a sudden he stops talking. At that moment, Irsay literally falls backward and passes out on the floor. Teddy's wife falls to the ground. I'm stunned, and Teddy is scrambling. He doesn't know whether to pick up his wife or Irsay first. It's crazy, everybody is scrambling, and now everybody is staring at what's going on.

Bob Terpening (aka the Doughnut Thief), who's been with Irsay since the Colts were in Baltimore, hustles over and looks at me. He says, "Help me pick him up?" Now, this is getting a little embarrassing, but okay,

I'll help the owner up. Terpening tells me to help get Irsay in the house. I'm like, "What the fuck are you talking about?" He can't handle Irsay himself, so he tells me, "Just do it." So now I'm helping carry Irsay out of the room. As I'm walking, Terpening and I have Irsay arm-in-arm, just dragging his feet along. The other players see me and start doing the smooching sound and snickering at me that I'm a kiss-ass. Yeah, this is just great—my freaking drunk-ass owner is making me look like a jerk bag. Terpening and I get Irsay in the house, and I'm ready to go. Irsay had all these dogs too, and they all run up to us as we get in the house. Irsay is mumbling, "Look at my babies, they're so pretty." This shit is nuts. Terpening yells at me, "Help me get him to his bedroom." I'm like, "No way, this is as far as this goes. Next thing I know you're going to have me getting him out of his clothes or whatever. Fuck that. This is where the rescue mission ends."

Of course, my tight relationship with the owner evidently didn't mean much when it came time to talk about my contract. At one point after the 1993 season, my agent Gus Sunseri comes down to Indy, and we're supposed to sit down and get a new contract. I come into the room, and I've got hospital scrubs on because I've just been at the hospital to get my right hand fixed—it was just a dislocated finger or something stupid like that. Sunseri and I tell them what I want, but Terpening, the guy negotiating the deal, looks at me and says, "You look fat to me." Whatever, asshole. I pull up my shirt, pound my gut, and say to him, "Hard as a rock." The guy says, "I'm telling you, you look fat." Fuck this guy. I get up, turn around, pull down my pants, and give him a full moon shot. Suffice to say, I didn't get a raise.

In 1993, Marchibroda's second season, we went backward again and ended up at 4–12. That season was also the end for Jeff George, the former number-one overall pick the year I came in. It got ugly for him in Indianapolis, which was weird, since he grew up there. He flipped off the fans at one point and argued with Marchibroda. After the season, he got traded to Atlanta in what was a pretty good deal for us. We got a bunch of draft picks.

The two best moves we made that year were bringing in Jim Harbaugh to be the quarterback and drafting running back Marshall Faulk. Both those guys were the real deal. Harbaugh, who has now become a damn good coach himself, wasn't the prettiest quarterback, but he was competitive as hell. Faulk was amazingly talented. For all that BS we went through with Dickerson, Faulk made up for it in a hurry. He came in, played hard, and played smart. From his very first game, you could just see how great he was going to be. As we were walking off the field I said to him, "Hey, rookie, sign your shoes and give them to me." Great guy, he actually did it, and the shoes are in my restaurant to this day in New Jersey.

We went 8–8 that season and got some momentum going. We were in just about every game, and you could see that Marchibroda was getting us in the kind of shape he wanted. Then, in 1995, we really got it cranked up, with Harbaugh leading us back in a bunch of games. They started calling him "Captain Comeback." We opened the season 3–0, winning those three games by a combined seven points. The rest of the year, practically every game was close. We had twelve of our sixteen games decided by a touchdown or less. It was crazy. We snuck into the playoffs with a win in the final game of the season.

This was my first time in the playoffs, and it was awesome. A big reason was that we had a great coaching staff that year. Marchibroda brought in Vince Tobin as the defensive coordinator, Greg Blache to coach the defensive line, and Jim Johnson (not Jimmy, but Jim) to coach the linebackers. Jim Johnson ended up being a great defensive coordinator later on, going to work in Philadelphia before he died of cancer. What a great teacher he was.

We opened the playoffs at San Diego. The Chargers had been in the Super Bowl the previous season, but we kicked their ass, 35–20. It was our most lopsided win of the year, and we did it without Faulk, which was even crazier. Zack Crockett, who had one carry the whole season, came in for Faulk and ran for 147 yards. Then we played Kansas City and beat them, 10–7, in a classic. I played with a horrible case of flu. We got four turnovers, and the Chiefs missed three field goals. Now we were in the AFC Championship Game with a chance to go to the Super Bowl. On top of that, we'd be playing in Pittsburgh, where I played college ball. This was awesome, and the game lived up to it. Another classic. We led the Steelers in the fourth quarter until Bam Morris scored on a one-yard touchdown run with 1:26 remaining in the game. Harbaugh almost pulled it out as he drove us to the Pittsburgh 29-yard line and threw a Hail Mary pass at the end that was almost caught.

Everything was looking up at that point. We had Faulk as a young star, Harbaugh as the quarterback, and plenty of other guys who were working their asses off. Then Marchibroda got forced out because they wanted to put Lindy Infante, the offensive coordinator, in charge. Marchibroda ended up going to Baltimore, which was strange, since that's where the Colts were originally from, but what a bunch of crap. Infante was a guy who only cared about whether his offense looked good or not. The reality is that Infante was just an average offensive coordinator, and none of us really understood why Jim Irsay made him the head coach. Jim Irsay was running the team day to day by that point, because his dad's health was declining. Everybody on that team would have died for Marchibroda. He was completely respected by the players. He was different and he was old-school in his approach, but he respected us and we loved him for it. He had just taken us to within one play of the Super Bowl and now Irsay forced him out?

It was probably the worst decision I have ever seen in the NFL—and trust me, I've seen a lot of stupid things that owners have done. Just because people have money doesn't mean they know what they're doing. Anyway, we get Infante running the show, even though none of the guys on defense respected the offense that much. We just killed those guys in practice every day. Infante would come over and complain about what we were doing. He'd start saying, "We have to slow it down so the offense looks good."

On top of that, Infante treated the players with no respect, especially any guy who got hurt. If you were injured, you were nothing to Infante. Football players are loyal to a guy until he's disloyal to them, and Infante was disloyal pretty fast to a lot of guys. He was the kind of guy who thought his coaching was better than our playing. As a coach, you have to respect your players, because those guys are the ones putting food on your table. That's how it works.

Of course, we had some things going right for a while. When we opened the 1996 season, we were still rolling pretty good. We won our first four games, including a one-point win at Dallas, which was huge. The Cowboys had beaten Pittsburgh in the Super Bowl after we lost to the Steelers, so it was kind of like our own chance to prove that we could have hung with those guys, and we did it. But then we lost four out of five before we got our shit together and won four of the last six games. We finished 9–7 and got into the playoffs for the second straight year.

Again, we had to go to Pittsburgh. However, by this time Infante was totally screwing with me. I didn't have any tolerance for his crap, so I told him plenty of times to his face that he wasn't handling stuff right. The guy was a bozo. You know me, always the politician. I'd look right at him and say, "Your offense sucks, why don't you work on scoring a couple of points?" Oh, he hated me.

That season I had torn some cartilage in my knee and missed six games. They didn't think there was a problem because they couldn't see anything on the tests. I was telling our team doctor, Shelbourne, that I knew there was a problem. After surgeries on both my knees, I knew those joints pretty well. I kept telling him and telling him that I had a chunk of cartilage in my knee. Finally, he goes in and actually finds the chunk of cartilage. He was pretty shocked when he found it.

Anyway, I'm ready to play in the playoffs, but Infante just wants to screw with me, so they make me inactive and tell me I'm not going to make the trip for the playoff game. What? I'm not playing or traveling to a playoff game? Infante doesn't even have the guts to tell me. Instead, he has the PR guy tell me. I'm one of the captains, and he's pulling this crap. So I say to myself, *All right, my contract is about to run out with these assholes, so I'll just fly to Pittsburgh myself.* They don't know what I'm doing, and they don't realize that I'm on the list of players who are supposed to interview with the network the night before the game. You're supposed to tell the game analysts about what's going on and what to look for. So I go in there and tell them everything that's going on with the team. The network guys are eating it up. They tell me, "Oh, stick around, we'll give you passes so you can sit in the TV booth with us." I say, "Okay," and then I walk out of the meeting.

As I'm leaving, here comes Lindy Infante with the PR director. They go, "What the fuck are you doing here?" I say, "I just did the meeting, and I told them every fucking thing, that you didn't fly me out, that you're a scumbag, that you're an idiot." Infante flips out because he knows he's busted now. So then they chase me down and say, "We've got a penthouse suite for you at the hotel, we're going to pay for everything. We wanted you here." I completely call Infante out. I say, "No, you didn't, and don't act like you did. I'm going to stay on Pittsburgh's sideline, even during the game, as a matter of fact. How about that?" Then, when Infante calls me after the Colts get their asses kicked, he wants me to sign back with the Colts. I tell him, "Go fuck yourself. You treat me like that and you want me?" That was the demise of my days in Indy. Great town, great fans, I loved it there, but I wasn't playing another down for that guy.

GOOSE TALES WITH . . .
TED MARCHIBRODA

Ted Marchibroda was Tony Siragusa's favorite coach in the NFL, a man who brought discipline and direction to the Indianapolis Colts and who Siragusa later followed to Baltimore. As with everything involving Siragusa, there were some bumps along the way. Or at least Siragusa was bumping into something.

"I saw Goose recently at a game. It was me, Goose, and Brad Seely, who is now the special teams coach with San Francisco and was our special teams coach in Indianapolis when I first got there. We were all standing out on the field before the game, and Brad said, 'Coach, do you remember when Goose ran into that snowplow in New York?' That's the most humorous thing I can think of as far as Goose, and there are a lot of humorous things. We're in New York to play the Jets, and it had snowed on Friday and Saturday. The snow was in big piles along the sideline, and they had a snowplow over to the side. So as the game is going on, Goose is chasing the Jets quarterback along the field toward the sideline. The quarterback sidesteps him, or just stops, and lets Goose run past him. Goose can't stop, and he keeps on going. You have to remember, he has a lot of momentum going, and you can't stop something that big. It's like how it takes a mile for a train to come to a full stop. So he's going, and he runs right into the snowplow, does the face plant into the thing. His whole body hits the thing, and he just plants right into the thing. It's not very often you can say that something stopped Goose, but I think the snowplow stopped him.

"Not everybody really saw it at the time, so one of the things I would do for our film review of the game the next week is that I would show some of the outstanding plays of the game and some of the humorous incidents. You have to break it up a little and keep it lively. When the players saw this—it was selected as one of the humorous incidents, naturally—it was the funniest thing you ever saw. Everybody laughed, and they said, 'Run it again, run it again, run it again.' It was one of those kinds of things. They couldn't get enough of it, and Goose was great about it because Goose can laugh at himself. He was able to laugh at that, which is good for your whole team. A lot of players can't laugh at themselves, but if they see somebody else do it, it's a little easier.

"I think early on in his career, Goose wasn't quite ready to play in the NFL. Goose is a fun-loving guy, and I don't think he was ready to commit himself totally to playing. If you wanted to have a good time at night, you followed Goose. But we had this one incident where I thought I really won Goose over. We used to weigh the guys in every week. I don't remember exactly how much you were fined at the time, but it was so much per pound if you were overweight. Then, if you were overweight the next week, the fine doubled. Maybe it was $50 a pound and jumped to $100, something like that. Again, I don't recall the specifics, but guys didn't like to get fined. Nobody likes to get fined, no matter how much or how little it is.

"Anyway, Goose was fined, and then he was fined again and I doubled it, but this went on and on for about three or four weeks, so it was getting expensive. Then one day he walks in my office, and he says, 'Coach, I'm trying to do this. I'm trying to keep my weight down and come in properly, but I can't. I just can't do it.' The other thing is that not all those guys were making a lot of money back then, so this was getting costly. So I say, 'Okay, Goose, I'm not going to double your fine,' because I could visualize it coming into $800, $1,600, or even $3,200 if this kept going. I went so far as to stop fining him altogether. The rea-

My dad on the old gridiron.

I can't tell you how popular
John Travolta was back then.

My loving parents.

I was a cute kid once.

King of the mat!

After a tough game in high school.

My first stab at an acting career.

Young love—my wife, Kathy, and I.

Here comes the groom.

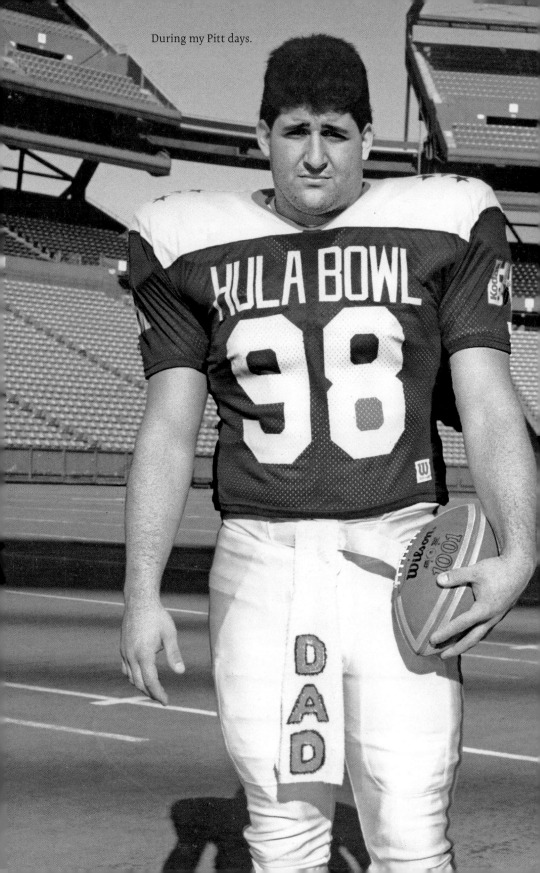

During my Pitt days.

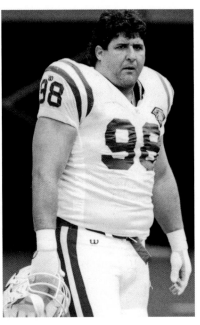

Some tough seasons in Indy.

But I tried to keep my sense of humor.

On top of the world! COURTESY OF GETTY IMAGES

Coach and I at the end of the Super Bowl. COURTESY OF GETTY IMAGES

Hosting my radio show in Baltimore.

My setup on the sidelines for calling games.

On the set of *Man Caves* with Jason Cameron. COURTESY OF GETTY IMAGES

My crew.

son I did it, and I told him this: 'I believe you, Goose. I believe you that you're trying and that you can't make it.'

"I think this is what turned things around for him—finally somebody believed him about his weight. Many of the other coaches that he had were always saying, 'Well, you know, he's overweight, he's not playing as well as he can just because of the fact of his weight.' But he played extremely well, he became serious, he became one of our leaders. He's a very smart football player, which again, once he started to learn, once he got involved in it, he really took over. Really, I think that's all it took with Goose, just saying, 'I believe in you,' and he just took off as a player and became one of our leaders. He's a great guy in the locker room. You love to have him on your team; he's that type of a guy, really.

"Before that, he wasn't quite ready to settle down yet. He had to go through that period of time when you're having a good time, really letting your hair down, which most everybody does in the NFL until they realize, 'Hey, this is a job, I've got to work at it.' Once he did, he became a real football player.

"We had this one game, I can't exactly remember when it was, but we played a horrible first half. We didn't play well at all. So at halftime, I was giving a little speech, talking about how we had to do whatever it took to get back in this game, really throw ourselves into it. As I was finishing up and we were getting ready to go back out, Goose just turned over this big table with Gatorade all over it. He was really upset at that moment, and I think he wanted to make sure we had everybody's attention. We came back and won that game, and I think that was an incident that helped us get ready to play the second half. Right there, he became a leader. He didn't have to say much, he just had to show it. He had that fire and passion, and he was finally showing it to people because he realized how important this was. He became a leader."

08

FROM LOW-
BALLED TO
BALTIMORE

So in March 1997, after seven years in Indianapolis, I finally had a chance to hit free agency and make some money. After the blowup with Lindy Infante, there was no way I was going back to Indy. Though I was tempted to follow Ted Marchibroda to Baltimore, which was obviously close to home, this was my chance to shop myself around the league for a good deal, and I was going to take that opportunity and do a little traveling around the country.

In one of the great ironies of all time, my first stop was Oakland, where I got to meet with the late, great Hall of Famer Al Davis. First of all, Davis was a little different. Actually, he was kind of a nut job, talking and talking and talking. I'm like, "Al, do you want me or not? Make me an offer already." Eventually, he makes me an offer, but I have to run the numbers a little, because California is crazy. You've got like a 10 percent state tax and then all these other taxes—it's a lot. So I'm doing the numbers, and I say, "I'll let you know in the morning." So the next day comes, and I have to wait the whole morning because Al likes to sleep till noon.

Finally, Al comes in and goes, "Every day is a new day, and I want to offer you $50,000 less." I was like, "Excuse me, you want to do what?" Well, for the second time in like two months I'm telling somebody to go fuck himself. After I tell Al that, I tell him to give me a plane ticket. I'm out of here.

Seriously, he said, "Every day is a new day." If you're much of a football fan, you probably remember what happened in the 2000 playoffs. We rolled into Oakland for the AFC Championship Game, and I got the big hit on Rich Gannon that knocked him out of the game, sending Baltimore to the Super Bowl where we would get the championship that Davis so desperately wanted. After I hit Gannon and saw Davis after the game, I said, "You should have spent the $50,000, you dumb-ass."

After I leave Oakland and get home, I get a call from Cincinnati. Dick LeBeau, another Hall of Famer, is the head coach of the Bengals at the time, and he's interested in me. Anyway, the Bengals tell me they have a ticket waiting for me at the airport to go to Cincinnati. Sweet, so I go to the airport, and the Bengals have a coach ticket waiting for me. Seriously, I'm 340 pounds or whatever, and they leave me a coach ticket. So I go back to the girl at the counter, and I say, "This is a coach ticket. Is it refundable?" She says yes, so I refund it and get $450, cool. I head back to the house, get a couple of cocktails, buy some beer and drink that, and have a nice time. Of course, the media in Cincinnati is expecting me, so they call me and ask, "Where are you?" I tell them exactly what happened—the Bengals bought me a coach ticket and I cashed it in. Then I say, "Look, I'm not coming. You want to sign me to a multimillion-dollar contract and you send me a coach ticket? Are you kidding me?" The media goes crazy with all the stories about how the team is so cheap. So the Bengals call me back and say, "Okay, we'll get you a first-class ticket."

So I fly out there and meet LeBeau. He picks me up and takes me around. I hear all the stories from the other players about how they only have one kind of tape and you can only get one pair of socks during the season, how cheap the organization is. I give LeBeau a lot of credit; he's trying hard to get me to join the team. He's a great dude. So we go to dinner—me, LeBeau, and a couple of players. I can't remember who they were, but they're acting all uptight around the coach. They're young guys, so when the waitress walks up and asks if anybody wants something to drink, this young guy says, "I'll have a Coke." The next guy says the same thing. The waitress asks me, and I say, "Yeah, give me a beer and two shots of Jack Daniel's." LeBeau goes next. He smiles and says, "I'll have what Goose is having." The young guys try to change their order, and I say, "No, no, you guys get your Coke or your Sprite, you pussies."

I could tell LeBeau loved me right off the bat. But I just knew that he wasn't going to be there that long. It was the Bengals; no coach ever survived. At least not until after we helped get my boy Marvin Lewis a job there a few years later. I'll explain that later.

So after that trip is done, I go to Baltimore to sit down with Marchibroda. Like I said, I love Teddy. Good guy, straight shooter. In the one season he had been with the Ravens, the team went 4–12. They weren't very good, but you could see they had some young studs, like Jonathan Ogden at left tackle and Ray Lewis at linebacker. The place was still a little chaotic because they had just moved from Cleveland. Man, when they left

Cleveland—that was a shit storm around the league. Now, they're still trying to get past all that crap, so they need some more veteran leadership. That's what Marchibroda wants from me. They already have Rob Burnett, a defensive end who ended up being one of my closest friends ever. They have Vinny Testaverde, a good Italian quarterback with a big arm. Marchibroda tells me, "This is your kind of place. You need to help me rebuild. We've got some problems in the locker room we have to fix first, but we can win here." You know he hooks me.

He brought in me and Mike McCrary, a great guy who was a huge hustler and tough guy on the outside. All they needed was another defensive tackle, and they got Larry Webster. Then they brought in Sam Adams, who was a challenge, but by the time he showed up in 2000 we were all set. We were so set that we could handle Sam and all his crap.

But we really did need to fix the locker room. After I signed, we have one of those off-season minicamps, and a bunch of the players don't want to practice on Sunday. They want the extra day off. So a couple of the guys stand up and say they're not going to go to work that day, they aren't showing up. I'm thinking, *What the hell is wrong with you guys? Are you out of your freaking minds? The coach said we have to go to practice. You can't not go.* But they all stick together—what am I supposed to do? I can't go against the other players, or it's going to divide the locker room even more. So I go to see Marchibroda, and I say, "Ted, all the guys decided, I can't go against them." He says, "I know, but those guys won't be here next year. You don't worry about it, just work on cleaning up the locker room. Those guys who don't want to work, they're going to be gone soon enough."

That was music to my ears. Every guy who was a problem, Marchibroda got rid of him. He fired them all and started bringing in more and more of the right guys, and then it was my locker room. I could start saying, "This is what we're going to do. Coach wants us to practice, we'll go practice." It got bumpy sometimes, because Marchibroda was great at bringing in guys with really strong character—guys who believed in themselves and what they were doing.

Marchibroda didn't do it alone. I also have to give Baltimore general manager Ozzie Newsome a lot of credit for the turnaround. For people who don't know football that well, Newsome is probably the best GM in the business. And a big reason why is, he's not only a former player, he's a Hall of Fame player who really understands how a team works. You're not just putting together a bunch of talented people. You're building a group that wants to work together, that loves each other. I'm not being corny about this. To me, it's like all those guys I grew up with back in Kenilworth. I could call those guys today, and they would show up with baseball bats to help me get out of a problem. We're talking about building a bond between people.

When I first got to Baltimore, we had a pretty good offense going with Testaverde and Marchibroda working together, but the defense couldn't stop anybody. Seriously, everybody remembers that 2000 Baltimore defense that set all the records and led us to the Super Bowl, but back in 1997, when I first got there, we were all over the place on defense.

What changed was that we started to get more and more guys who really respected themselves first. Football is a great game because it says a lot about players' pride and respect in themselves. Seriously, you're tested play after play after play to see what you have in yourself, and everybody around you sees it. On every play you have something to prove to the guy next to you so that he can trust you—so he knows you're going to have his back—and vice versa. You've almost got to love each other, and you've got to trust each other. I think trust is the biggest thing you've gotta have in football, because you can't do it by yourself—nobody can. In Baltimore we were misfits; we were all screwed up somehow. But it didn't matter because we had trust. I don't care if you're a great player, if you're a medium player, or if you're a crap player. I just gotta know who you are and what you're going to do. Because if I don't know what you're going to do, and you do the wrong thing at the wrong time, then I can't trust you. You're going to let everybody down.

That includes coaches. I talked about Marvin Lewis before. He was our defensive coordinator when I got there, and he stayed all the way through our Super Bowl year. He eventually became the head coach in Cincinnati. (If you coach defense in Baltimore, you have a pretty good shot at being a head coach, as Lewis, Rex Ryan, Mike Smith, and Jack Del Rio have shown.) Anyway, when I first got there, one of the problems was that Marvin had five hundred plays designed for the defense. It was unbelievable. Now, Marvin is one smart dude, but when you have eleven people all moving around, the idea isn't to be more complicated from the start—it's to be less complicated. So I looked at Marvin one day and said, "Marv, you gotta tone this down." He understood where I was going. He took it down to where everybody knew what they were doing. Make it simple first, and then you can get complicated after you know what everybody around you is going to do. Not only did we have guys who were still young, like Ray Lewis in his second season, but we had a bunch of rookies who were trying to just figure out what the NFL was about. We had Peter Boulware and Jamie Sharper, two of our linebackers, out there as rookies. We had a rookie safety in Kim Herring. And all the while, Marvin was trying to put more plays in until we said, "Enough."

That season we got torched a few times. The Steelers put up forty-two on us in the sixth week. That sucked, but it wasn't nearly as bad as later in the season when they kicked our ass 37–0. Still, as the season was going on, we started to get it. We finished 6–9 that year, but we were learning about each other. Our record was pretty much the same the next season in 1998; we finished 6–10, but you could get the sense we were getting closer. We signed Rod Woodson, a Hall of Famer who was playing safety by then, and we drafted Duane Starks to play cornerback, so we were getting better in the secondary in a hurry. We played Pittsburgh tough that year. You could just tell things were moving along.

The only problem was, the offense started to go backward a little bit. We lost Testaverde and replaced him with Jim Harbaugh, who I had played with in Indianapolis. Again, tough guy, good leader, but he was getting close to the end by this time. With the offense struggling, Marchibroda lost his job, which pretty much sucked. We brought in Brian Billick, this guy who was supposed to be an offensive genius. He had been with Minnesota for five years, putting up all sorts of numbers. Of course, they had some pretty good players too, like Randy Moss, Robert Smith, and Cris Carter, plus a damn good offensive line. I think I could have coached them well too.

So Billick came in and was a pretty confident guy, but he was good for our team in a lot of ways. First, he let men be men, which I respect. He didn't put a lot of rules on us. He expected us to conduct ourselves like pros and police ourselves. Second, he didn't mess with the defensive staff. He left Marvin Lewis to coach the defense and left the rest of the staff pretty much alone. He did bring in his brother-in-law, Mike Smith, but Mike was a quality guy. He really knew his stuff and did his homework.

Unfortunately, by 1999 Harbaugh was gone, so now we were really starting to scramble at quarterback. But the defense was just humming along. In the first round in 1999, we drafted cornerback Chris McAlister, so now we had him, Woodson, and Starks. That was nice, and we took some really serious strides that season. We opened up with a loss to St. Louis, which sucked because the Rams were starting some no-name guy who had been all over the world in NFL Europe and the Arena League and even worked as a bag boy in a grocery store. Maybe you've heard of the guy . . . Kurt Warner. Who knew? He lit us up for 309 yards and three touchdowns, and we lost, 27–10. He went on to win the Most Valuable Player Award, and the Rams won the Super Bowl.

We actually weren't too bad in that game. The Rams scored thirty or more points in twelve games during the regular season and didn't score less than twenty-one in any other game in the regular season. Plus, they ended up playing Tennessee in the Super Bowl that season. At the time, the Titans were in our division, so we played them twice a year. The first time we played, they beat us, 14–11. Then we played them again in December and slapped them around for a 41–14 victory. Looking back at it, we were really good in those games, and that showed how far we had come. We finished the season 8–8. We won five of our final seven games, and four of our losses were by three points or less. At the time, we were playing in the loaded AFC Central, where not only did we have Tennessee, which had Steve McNair and Eddie George and went 13–3, and traditionally good Pittsburgh, but we had a really good Jacksonville team. Jacksonville, which had Mark Brunell, Jimmy Smith, and Fred Taylor, actually won the division at 14–2 before getting knocked out of the playoffs in the AFC Championship Game by Tennessee. So when you think about it, going 8–8 was pretty good. We lost twice to Jacksonville, once by a touchdown and the other time by a field goal.

The key was that we were starting to figure each other out. We had three years of playing together—not just playing together, but really getting to know each other, on the field and in the locker room. Again, I talk about trust. Now, if you read what my man Rob Burnett wrote about our time there, it wasn't always easy. Trust me, we had some real brawls in our place, especially once Sam Adams got there with his weird mood swings. But that was part of it. Football pushes you in every way possible, physically and emotionally. You really have to trust each other. I'll get back to that more when I talk about our championship season.

And you have to build to that point. I see all these teams now where people expect it's going to happen right away. It's like the Philadelphia Eagles in 2011, when they brought in all these guys and called them "the Dream Team." In 1995, back when I was playing in Indianapolis, Miami did the same thing when they brought in all these star players, something like twenty former first-round picks, and tried to win it all. Guess what happened? Those teams played like crap. The Eagles, who had Michael Vick, couldn't get it together. The Dolphins, even with my man Dan Marino, couldn't get on the same page. Everybody wanted to be the star.

It doesn't work that way. Not everybody can be that guy. If you have a really good team, everybody gets a chance to be that guy from time to time, but you can't be the star every game. It's the nature of the game, particularly if you really want to be good. In football, if the other team wants to take somebody away, I don't care how good they are, they can take them away. It doesn't matter if you're Jerry Rice or Randy Moss or Barry Sanders—if the other team wants to stop one guy, they can do that. You watch the way Bill Belichick coaches: that's what his teams do when they're good. They take away the other team's best player. It's pretty simple. The question is, can the rest of your team make enough plays to make up for that?

That's what our defense had to learn to do. We had stars like Ray Lewis and Woodson. What the rest of us had to do was do our part. We had to be ready to make a play when our time came. We had to trust in each other that some guy wasn't going to go off the reservation when the time came. That's what I mean about love and trust. I gotta love the guy next to me enough to give him that chance when the time comes to make a play, and I gotta trust that he's going to do the same for me. It ain't easy. You have a lot of egos in a locker room. You have a lot of guys who have been the man—the stud, the star—their whole life. All of a sudden, they can't be that guy all the time. They have to allow somebody else to shine.

The lucky part for us was, we had a lot of great players who didn't necessarily get the respect they deserved right off the bat. I went undrafted. Burnett was a fifth-round draft pick out of Syracuse who played fourteen years in the NFL and made it to the Pro Bowl. Mike McCrary was drafted in the seventh round and made the Pro Bowl and All-Pro. Yeah, we had a lot of first-round picks: Ray Lewis, McAlister, Starks, Woodson, Peter Boulware, and eventually Sam Adams. But we also had guys who could have or should have been first-round picks, but also knew what it was like to have to bust your ass to make a team and get recognized. You need both types to have a really great team. At least you need to have both types of attitude.

By the end of the 1999 season, Marvin Lewis had gotten his great ideas under control. He wasn't calling five hundred plays, he was calling the ones that really worked for us. He also trusted us when we changed things. A lot of the time, Marvin would call something really complicated and we'd say, no, no, just line up and keep it simple. We'd see the offense come to the line, and we'd look at each other. I'd look at McCrary, who played defensive end next to me a lot, and say, "Mac, look at the quarterback, I got your back." McCrary would take off, *boom*, gone. I might say to him or somebody else, "I'm just going to bull rush, make sure there's nothing to my side." *Boom*, I'd get a sack. It was like, hey, we've got something here. We started to really know each other. We'd say to Jamie Sharper or Peter Boulware, get on the outside and make sure you're rushing. We'd give Mike the inside move. Once Peter or Jamie distracted the left tackle, *boom,* the door was open for Mike to get the quarterback. I just had to make sure the guard couldn't step out on him. That's what I'm talking about with teamwork, with trust, with love for the guys you work with.

I see the other side of it all the time. You see guys who just want to get sacks so they can make money, or get women, or do whatever drives them. They don't give a shit about playing together with the other guys around them. That's why teams don't win a lot of the time. It's not because they don't have talent. It's because one guy starts playing for himself, and the rest of the guys start following that same path. Pretty soon, nobody is doing the right thing. It's a mess. We had that same type of thing happen during training camp one year. We had a guy who was in camp with us, a pretty talented guy. He might have made the team. But in the middle of camp, he just quit. He didn't want to do it anymore. No problem, that's fine. Football ain't for everybody, we all get it.

Later in the season, we got a couple of injuries, and Ozzie Newsome, our GM, thought about bringing this guy back. The kid was talented, and he wanted to give it another try. That was fine, but it wasn't going to be with us. We went to Ozzie and said, "Look, Ozzie, if you want to bring him back, that's fine, but you better hope he can play the entire defensive line by himself because he's going to be the only guy you have." That guy quit on us, and there was no way he was going to be welcome in our room again. I don't care how good you are: if you quit on our group, a bunch of guys who are willing to accept anybody—good, bad, or indifferent—for what they are as long as they play hard, then fuck you. You don't belong with us. I give Ozzie a lot of credit. He could have called us on it and tried to stuff this guy up our ass. He didn't, he got it. He totally understood where we were coming from. We would have rather had some guy off the street who couldn't play a lick as long as he was dedicated. Give me a guy who wants to fight with the guy next to him and I'll show you an army. That's how we worked.

The other key element to our team came along in 1999: Rex Ryan, our defensive line coach, and eventually the defensive coordinator after Marvin Lewis left. Yep, Rex, who is now ripping it up with the New York Jets. Ryan was great for us. He was like the final piece that kept the group moving forward. In fact, he was particularly good when we got Sam Adams because he was able to deflect so much of Sam's bullshit. He set a good example for us when we had our run-ins with Sam. I'll get to it later, but that was some complicated shit. Rex has the perfect temperament: he wants to be great, and he wants to have fun. With Rex, coming to work is fun, for him and the players both. A lot of things about football really suck. Practice sucks. Sitting in meetings for hours and hours sucks. Look, we're all a bunch of restless, aggressive people. You think we really want to be sitting there going over tendencies for hours and hours? It's like any job. The difference is that game day is such a high, such a great experience. All the rest of the crap you do to get there just sucks. What Rex did was make that part of it fun. Plus, he had a really good pulse for the room. He just knew when guys needed to be pushed, or when we had to throttle down a little to get through the BS part of the season. Look, you get to week six or seven of an NFL season and it's rough. You still have a long way to go, and everybody is crabby. Everybody in the room is banged up. You've been at it since the end of July when training camp started. You need somebody to get the room going. Rex was that guy.

Just trust me when I say everybody had everybody else's back—right to the most extreme moments, and I can attest to that. I'll illustrate with a good story from our championship season. Well, the word *good* is relative. In this case, "good" is not comfortable.

One season in Baltimore, the night before a midseason game against the Redskins, I wake up at like 5:00 A.M. with a stomachache that is so painful, it hurts just to have anyone touch my skin. It feels like my lower GI system is ready to explode. I'm sweating, I've got a headache, and my body is just doing something that's not normal. So I call our trainer, Bill Tessendorf, and he says he'll get the doctor and take a look at me. The game isn't until 1:00 P.M. I would usually get to the stadium about three hours before, around 10:00 A.M., but this day it's 8:00 A.M. and I'm already at the stadium, waiting to get an X-ray. They come back after the X-ray and tell me that the only problem is, I'm constipated like there's no to-morrow. It's like my entire intestinal tract is filled with crap, literally. Okay, what am I supposed to do? I'm sitting in the training room, it's about 9:00 A.M. by now, and they're giving me a couple of great ideas. Either I can take a serious laxative (but they have no idea when I'm going to let loose), or they can give me an enema. Oh great, this is some choice.

So I go with the enema. By this time, the only other player in the locker room is our kicker, Matt Stover, and I'm not too fond of kickers by nature. So I go over to the bathroom stall, and the doctor is starting to put on gloves. I'm like, "Dude, give me the tube, you're not shoving a tube in my butt. I'll do it myself." So they give me this little rubber tube, and it's got gel on it. Wow, this is going to be fun. Anyway, the doctor starts to squeeze the water into me, and now the pain is just getting worse. The doctor is telling me to hold it in as long as I can. Stover is over there, tak-ing a leak, and saying, "Come on, dude." I yell at him, "Dude, don't tell me about what the hell I have to do to take a crap."

Before I go on with this story, I'll admit that I probably deserved a lit-tle shit from Stover, so to speak. Again, my approach with kickers is, they are to be tolerated. It's like with little kids: they should be seen but not heard. You always see them at practice with their toy-store shoulder pads, running around and never hitting anybody or getting hit. I don't even know why they show up for practice; all we do is make up shit for them to do. Then, if the game is on the line, they have to be left alone like they're golfers or something. There is this unwritten rule that if you're lining up for a game-winning field goal, you're not supposed to talk to your own kicker. Fuck that—I used to go up to Stover and tell him, "Listen, you shitbag little kicker, you better make that kick, or don't come back to the sideline. I'll break your fucking skinny legs if you miss it. Think I'm kidding? Just go do your fucking job." One time I think I yelled at him, "If you miss this kick, I'll hurt your family." Hey, you had to toughen 'em up. Stover never said a word to me, never even blinked. I think I got a smile out of him once when I threatened his family. I love Stover. We wouldn't have made the Super Bowl without him. But I hate the idea of kickers on principle.

So back to the backed-up bowel story. So as I'm taking the enema, I hold it in and hold it in, just praying this is going to alleviate some of the pain. Finally, I sit down and let it go. Nothing, just pure water. What the hell is going on here? Now I'm really pissed off. Other players are coming in, the coaches are there, Billick is asking if I'm going to play or if I have to be inactive. I've never been inactive for something like this in my whole career. So now they're going to do another freaking enema. They tell me, "We didn't put enough water in the first time." I'm like, *Are you kidding me?*

The doctor gets another IV bag. I grab the hose again, and away we go. He puts like three-quarters of the bag in me. Holy crap, this hurts. Stover, who's this skinny shit and must weigh all of ninety-eight pounds, is trying to tell me to calm down. I just want to kill him because he's saying, "Look, this is what you've got to do." I just want to break him in half. I say, "If you don't stop talking, I'm going to end up in jail for murder." Freaking kickers. Plus, with all the players now around, this is getting embarrassing. So finally, I go back in the stall, and *whoosh,* everything comes out. I look down and all that's come out is like a grape. *Are you kidding me?* So everybody is looking at me and asking, "Can you play?" I'm thinking, *I just took two enemas and I'm still in pain—how the hell am I going to do this?* All I can think of is, *I'm going to go out there and crap my pants.*

Now, there are a lot of disgusting things that happen on a football field. Guys throw up, guys piss down their leg, they get nasty injuries, and all sorts of other stuff. But you have to believe me when I say that this could have been the most disgusting thing I ever witnessed, involving either me or somebody else.

But you know me—I'm a problem-solver and I'm going to play. Again, this is our big year. Our defense is great, and I'm going to do whatever I can to get on the field. Then I find out this is one of the days when we're wearing white pants. White jersey, white pants—all white. We have black pants and purple pants, but this has to be the day we wear white. Fuck. So I go back to Tessendorf, and I tell him, "Dude, if I go down and I'm lying on the ground and I'm on my back in severe pain, do not turn me over. Whatever you do, don't turn me over. Just call for the stretcher, put that thing underneath me, and you get me inside, because I just shit in my pants. You know the camera is going to be on me, so don't you dare turn me over. I'm serious."

Now, I'm sitting at my locker and every guy on the team is coming up saying, "Are you okay?" Yeah, yeah, I'm fine, leave me the hell alone. I'm just thinking to myself, *I can't crap my pants. What the hell can I do?* I go to the equipment guys, and they have this like two-sided carpet tape. What they use that for is to stick it on your pads and then stick your jersey to it so that people can't grab your uniform as easy. Well, I have a different idea. I take some of the tape and stick it between my butt cheeks and basically tape my ass shut. I gotta dam this thing up somehow. Then I take some regular athletic tape and start taping it around my butt. Finally, I put on my uniform, but I can't even put my belt on because the pain is so bad.

As it turned out, I didn't need to take those precautions, and everything ended up being okay as far as that was concerned. After the game, everything cleared up nicely. The only problem was, I made the bus back to Baltimore wait a little long. Then I used the story for fodder on my radio show. Look, I'm a guy who can laugh at himself. But there's one thing I never told anybody: that game really hurt my pride because, on one of the key plays, I couldn't move and the Redskins made a big play that cost us the victory. That bugged me for a long time. It still does, really, because my teammates couldn't depend on me. Yeah, I had an excuse, but that's not the point: you can't have excuses. You have to get the job done. Nobody gives a damn about whether you're constipated or whatever the hell it is. You just have to get the job done. That's how every guy on our team was, particularly on the defense.

09

THE ART OF CHEATING

When I talk about the art of cheating, I ain't talking about the stupid shit that happens at the bottom of a pile after a fumble. By this time, we all know that crap. You see forty-five guys pile on top of each other, stuff happens. Sometimes it looks like the guys who aren't even in the game jump in there to get some action. The point is, yeah, you're trying to do whatever you can to get the ball. I mean, whatever you can do. You try to break a guy's fingers, you grab his balls, you poke his eyes, everybody knows that crap, and that's not smart-guy stuff.

That's just brute force shit—how much pain can you inflict on another guy to get the ball back. The only important thing about the piles is to make sure your quarterback is never near them. But any dummy who plays can figure that out. It's like with this big bounty controversy they had in the NFL with the New Orleans Saints. I just think to myself, what a bunch of idiotic crap. You mean to tell me that if I'm making $1 million or $2 million per year and you pay me an extra $1,000 or $1,500, I'm going to hit a guy that much harder? Are you serious?

I didn't need extra cash to go hit someone hard. You think a couple of dollars are going to make me want to hurt somebody? The game is violent to begin with, and that's the point. When I played, I didn't care if my mother was out there, if she had the ball, she was going to get hit. Now, I'm not going out there to hit somebody's knee. That's not the point, but it's a violent game.

The only time it changes is if somebody is trying to hurt somebody else. If you go after my knee, I'm damn sure going to come after yours. If you hurt me intentionally, I damn sure expect my guys to go after you. If you cross that line, that's the way it is. If you chop a guy and you keep doing it, as soon as there's an interception and the ball is going the other way, I'm going for both your knees on the return. I remember going into games, watching film of how guys played, and saying, "That's a guy who will cross the line." You have to watch out for guys like that.

Again, it was only in retaliation. I never started anything like that, and I never had a bounty system like what they did in New Orleans on any team I played for. We all have a mortgage to pay, so going outside the rules to hit somebody is wrong. But there were teams that would try. One year the NFL put together this video of what the officials should watch for on illegal blocks. There were like ten plays they showed. Eight of the ten must have been shots of the Raiders center and guard trying to cheap-shot me. The Raiders tried to chop me all the time. I wanted to kill those guys. I wanted to take them out to the parking lot and kick their asses.

Again, the bounty crap isn't what I'm talking about. That's idiot stuff. Even the coach who was in the middle of it, former New Orleans defensive coordinator Gregg Williams, he's the kind of guy who just does crazy shit all the time. If you watch sixty plays of his defense, forty-two of them are blitzes. He's just going after people all the time.

That's why it's stupid when I hear people react to this kind of stuff. There was some politician who said after the bounty story broke that Congress needed to look into football and the illegal activity. Come on, dude, don't be an idiot. There is a world outside the perimeter of the field, and then there's the world between those lines. That's the only place where you can lay somebody out and you don't have to call an attorney.

You can look at the game, you can film it, you can study it, but unless you have the nuts to step on the field you're never going to understand it. You walk out there and you better have your head on a swivel, the umbilical cord cut, and your nuts dropping so that you're ready for what's going to happen. Otherwise, go play tennis. When I see people talking about the violence in the game and how there's too much of this and that, it aggravates me. I mean, really, what are we doing here? Football, at least the way I was brought up, requires a sense of intimidation. That's part of the game. Ronnie Lott wouldn't be in the Hall of Fame if it wasn't for that.

Back to the quarterbacks for a second. I don't like many quarterbacks, but you do have to protect that guy a little. Hell, you saw what happened to Eli Manning during a game against Philadelphia in 2011. He threw an interception and just kind of meandered toward the Eagles defensive players and *bam!* he got popped and knocked to the ground by a couple of Eagles players. Look, there's no mercy in this league. Same thing happened to Kurt Warner during the playoffs against New Orleans in 2009. He took one step toward a guy after losing the ball and got plowed. That was an old man out there. *Boom,* you're going down. Now, people think that was part of a bounty because it was the Saints, but really, go take a look at that play. Warner might have made a tackle if that guy hadn't hit him. That's the way the game has to be played.

When I talk about the art of cheating, I'm talking about the real inside stuff, the clever shit. For instance, if you didn't know already, there's a rule against putting Vaseline or silicone spray on your jersey. The reason is that linemen, particularly offensive linemen, used to use the stuff so that defensive linemen couldn't grab their jerseys too easily and just throw them around. As it is, it's pretty hard to grab a jersey. Players tend to wear them about four sizes too small so that when they put them on there's no excess for somebody to grab on to, which would make it that much easier to either throw them around on the line or tackle them.

Anyway, on top of the tight jersey, you'd get offensive linemen who'd once in a while use the Vaseline or the silicone. If they got caught, they'd have to come out of the game for a few plays and get a new jersey. The officials would then confiscate the jersey with the Vaseline or silicone on it and send it to the league, and the league would usually fine the guy a bunch of money. The Dolphins had this great situation back when Jimmy Johnson was coaching. One of their offensive linemen sprayed himself with silicone. He got caught by the officials, who took his jersey away and locked it in the officials' dressing room. While the game was going on, somebody from the Dolphins broke into the room and stole the jersey back. Great stuff.

Knowing what happens to these guys who use the spray, here's how I would twist it: If I was playing some guy who was particularly dirty, a cheap-shot artist, what I would do is put a bunch of Vaseline or silicone on my hands. Then I'd put the stuff all over his jersey and go to the ref and say, "Hey, he has some shit on his jersey, you better check that out."

The guy gets run from the game for two or three plays and then gets fined. That's good stuff too.

Hell, I was always trying to figure out some angle. When I was in Baltimore, we used to have this fishing tournament every spring. We'd have like twenty boats with all the players, and we'd fish for all kinds of stuff. They'd give out nice prizes—like big-screen TVs and all sorts of good stuff—for whoever caught the biggest fish. Of course, I'd be pretty competitive about this, and I'd have a couple of poles in the water. I'd catch a few, and then we'd head back to the docks and I'd look around. If I didn't have the biggest fish, well, I had a solution. I'd start stuffing the thing with the lead weights we had in the tackle boxes. I'd just keep stuffing and stuffing that fish until the freaking thing was full. Surprise, I won every year. My fish's belly might be all distended and shit, and it would frustrate the guys who walked up with all these big fish. The second time I won a TV, which I gave to Rex Ryan. Like I said, you have to know the angles.

What surprises me is when guys don't pick up on stuff like that more, especially with so much money on the line. It's like when they recently changed where the umpire stands. For most of the game now, the umpire stands behind the offensive line. They used to be behind the defensive line, but too many of those guys got hit with all the bodies flying around. Well, I can only imagine all the stuff I would get away with now if the umpire wasn't there. Oh my God, Ray Lewis would have run at the QB every play. I would be coming up with all sorts of ways to screw up the line. I'd be yelling "hut" all the time trying to copy the quarterback's voice. It would be nuts.

You look at some players like Ronde Barber, or when Sam Madison was playing toward the end of his career. Those guys are both cornerbacks, a position where you better be able to run like crazy, but by the time they were in their thirties, neither one of them could run very fast. You see Ronde Barber playing for Tampa Bay these days, and I would bet he couldn't run faster than a 4.7 in the 40-yard dash anymore. But he's really smart. As of when we wrote this book, he was in his fifteenth year, and he had played in every game since the second year of his career. He had forty-two interceptions and twenty-seven sacks (those are great numbers for a defensive back) and was playing good ball. You have to respect that. How does he do it? He knows the little tricks that go with playing. He knows the angles. He can diagnose a play in a hurry. Madison was the same way. He stuck around for twelve years in the NFL and finally won a title in his second-to-last season in 2007 with the New York Giants. He couldn't run a lick by the end, but he was damn smart. Want to know one of his best tricks? As he was running side by side with a wide receiver, he would be hitting the receiver on the thigh. That would slow down the receiver by keeping him from being able to bring his leg all the way up, totally messing with his stride. That used to drive wide receivers crazy. Great stuff. Most importantly, being smart like that kept those guys employed for a couple more years, making serious money.

I'd find little things like that all the time. Like in short-yardage situations, such as third-and-1, fourth-and-1, or maybe at the goal line. I specifically remember playing the Tennessee Titans, they're on the 1-yard line, and four seconds are left in the game. They have to get it in the end zone. They come to the line of scrimmage, and they all get ready. I see the quarterback's hands go underneath the center, and I yell, "Hut!" They fumble the ball. You pull that out once in a while during a game to get guys to jump or screw up a play. Of course, they have a rule against that, but you can still pull it out at critical times.

For instance, what you have to know is that the NFL wants games to run three hours, right on the nose, as much as possible. Look, you have to remember that this is entertainment. It's programming for the networks, and the networks like their programs to run on time—especially on a Sunday when you have 1:00 and 4:00 games. You have to keep those games on schedule, and part of how officials get graded is on whether they get the game run on time. Well, if a game is starting to run a little long, you better know as a player that you can get away with a little more. If the game started at 1:00 and it's almost 4:00, you can probably get away with an extra holding call or two because the refs want to get done. Trust me, I know, because their grade factors in on whether they get to work the playoffs or not. Now, we're talking about a lot of money for guys because refs get paid per game.

There was this one game where I pulled out the fake "hut" call three plays in a row. The offense is jumping and jumping, getting penalized. It's working perfectly. On the third one, the umpire is behind me, and he says, "You can't do that." I say, "Listen, dude, I know the rules. You can throw a flag one time. Unless you can verify that I yelled 'hut,' you're going to get downgraded. Now I'm going to the playoffs, this team's going to the playoffs. It depends on your rating whether you're going to go or not. I know I'm going to go, but if you keep throwing flags on me for yelling 'hut,' you're not going to go to the playoffs." I absolutely said that to him. I knew that we were getting tight on the three hours of game time, so he wanted to get done before going over three hours.

The point is, you have to have a really good sense of everything that's going on around you when you play the game. It's not just all about blocking and tackling and throwing and catching. There are other things going on, and you have to be able to manipulate things a little bit. There are also times you can distract the other team by being funny. It's like that son-of-a-bitch Brett Favre. Trust me, I love the guy. Probably one of the few quarterbacks I actually like. Still, he's a son-of-a-bitch. He used to get to the line and start calling his cadence. He'd be yelling, "Red 36, Red 36," or some shit like that, and all of a sudden he'd start talking during his cadence, like, "Red 36, everyone look at Goose's head, it doesn't fit in his helmet." He'd be making fun of me during the cadence, and it would just piss me off. I wanted to kill him, but that's part of the mind game. Favre was trying to distract me and everybody else during the game.

Trust me, there's all sorts of fun stuff like that happening during games. It's like me and Dan Marino used to talk all the time. We're both Italian and we both went to Pitt, as I mentioned before. We have a little brotherhood going. Anyway, early in my career, he noticed that when I got a sack, I would do this little flapping of my arms. Nothing crazy, just a little dip of my body and a flap of my arms; I tried to keep it subtle and smooth. I called it "The Goose," of course. He told me that was pretty cool, so I came back with a little bet: if I ever sacked him, he had to do "The Goose." He started talking shit to me about how there was no way I was ever going to sack him. Okay, I said, then bet me. I egged him on, and finally he bet me. Well, a few years later, after I get to Baltimore, he calls me the week before we play and says, "The bet's off. Our line is all banged up, the bet's off." I'm like, "What do you mean the bet's off?" Marino says, "No way, there's no way I can do 'The Goose' in front of my own team-mates, no way." Okay, well, we negotiated. I let him out of the bet for five dinners, and every dinner had to have this really nice bottle of wine on the table. I got him pretty good on that.

This other time, we're playing the Dolphins, and I'm rushing Marino and I kind of give him a shoulder around his waist, just a love-tap kind of thing. All of a sudden it's raining yellow penalty flags. You'd have thought I tried to assassinate Marino or something. You touch the guy and it's a federal crime. One of those dinners I got might have been my last meal, if you know what I mean. Well, I get penalized, and I'm sure I got fined for it. The next day, it's like eight in the morning, and I get this call. I answer and I hear, "Tony, this is Mrs. Marino, Danny's mom." I'm like, "Okay, hello?" She says, "I thought you and Danny were friends. What are you doing trying to take out his knees?" I get scolded by Marino's mom. Well, of course, I don't let this one go. The next time I'm with Danny at my golf tournament, I'm talking to the whole crowd, and I start talking about how Danny's mom called me. Remember, he owes me five dinners for the "Goose" bet, so he can't say anything. All he can do is admit it.

It's like all the stupid complaints you heard about Belichick and the Patriots during the "Spygate" crap back in 2007, when they got busted for videotaping signals. That kind of shit has been going on for years. Everybody is trying to get an edge on everything. But here's what I don't get: if I know that the other team is videotaping me (and it was no big secret back then), I would completely fuck with them. I would use dummy signals, I would change who's sending the signals, all sorts of shit to confuse them. It's just like the Vaseline trick—you have to fight fire with fire. Don't be a pussy and complain about how the other guy is cheating and it's wrong and all that shit—find a way to outsmart him. If he's dirty, you be dirtier. You know why? Because what the fuck is he going to say when he discovers that you're messing with him? "Oh, that guy is doing something deceptive to mess with us, after we stole his signals by videotaping him the previous game." Really, you think some coach is going to complain like that?

Don't get me wrong, I'm not defending Belichick. I'm just not going to wave a finger at him and say he was the only guy doing anything wrong—that's bullshit. And here's the other thing about the Patriots—what did they do after they got busted for supposedly cheating? They went 18-0 and came within a miracle finish by my dad's Giants of winning another Super Bowl and going 19-0. And along the way, they were killing people that season. Tom Brady threw for fifty touchdowns. That's obscene. You think they did that by cheating? Get outta here. They were damn good.

And they were damn good doing all the little smart things that I've been talking about. It's like the old classic way that you get extra time-outs, or you stop a team from using the no-huddle at will. You fake an injury. The thing is, you really have to sell it. I remember one time with the Patriots, Willie McGinest did that in a regular-season game in Indianapolis so the Patriots could get the right players on the field for a goal-line play. McGinest did it perfectly. Of course, thirty seconds later, he's standing on the sideline ready to go back in the game. The Patriots won the game, got home-field advantage for the AFC playoffs against the Colts, and rolled to another Super Bowl after Peyton Manning had so many problems throwing in shitty Boston winter weather. Those are the little tricks that go with playing, so that you can stop the clock without burning a time-out. Of course, the Giants kind of screwed it up in 2011 when they had two guys go down at the same time in a game. Look, you have to coordinate that stuff a little better. On most teams, you have one guy at a time who is designated to do that. You've got to know the ins and outs of the game. You've got to go and manipulate the game. Nobody does it better than Belichick.

There are things you can do as a player in a game if you are on the same page, and you gotta get a little bit of an advantage. That's all it takes. The other team may bitch and complain, but you have to have a little Hollywood in you to make sure you sell it. It's like on kickoff coverage. If you're running down trying to cover a kick and you're engaged with one of the blockers for a couple of seconds, just fall down at the end—it's virtually guaranteed you'll get a holding call that wipes out the return and puts the offense at like the 15-yard line to start. Officials can't look at every specific guy, but if they see a guy on the ground, they pretty much know he was held, so you have a great chance to get a flag—which is sometimes better than making the tackle. Particularly if the other team broke a big return and maybe scored. That could be the difference between winning and losing.

10

THE ROAD TO SUPER BOWL XXXV

If you know just a bit about football history, you know that our Super Bowl season in 2000 in Baltimore was a little different. It was a whole year of different, completely nuts. Of course, there was the Ray Lewis murder trial deal, which is a book unto itself. Then there was my holdout. Then there was our whole offense situation, which led to our quarterback situation. We survived it all because we had this unbelievable defense.

But at least for me, it almost never happened. This was the year when I got through the craziest and scariest freaking thing that ever happened to me. I was almost done as a football player. To explain, let me backtrack a little bit. Remember that I was talking about my bowel blockage story. Sorry to remind you of that, but it's sort of a setup to the next part of it. So I get through that game, and I'm talking about this whole thing on radio. It's hilarious the way I'm telling it, everybody on the radio show is cracking up, rolling on the floor, and the fans are going crazy with laughter. This is me at my best, telling over-the-top stories and making people laugh.

That week, we're hosting Tennessee, our division rival and the defending AFC champions. At the time, we're really rolling, even though we've just lost to Washington. We're 5–2, and we already have three shutouts. We've also already beaten Jacksonville, the team that won our division the year before with a 14–2 record; in fact, we've beaten them twice along the way. All our momentum from the end of the previous season is carrying over, and we've already won both our games that were decided by less than a touchdown. Yeah, we're coming off a loss and that sucks, but we know what we did wrong (me especially with the play I missed in that game). This game against the Titans is going to be huge, the kind of game that could propel us the whole season.

So after I tell half of Baltimore about my bowel problems, we get to the game on Sunday afternoon. Tennessee has this great offensive line with Hall of Famer Bruce Matthews at center, a couple of tough guards in Benji Olson and Zach Piller, and a pretty good left tackle in Brad Hopkins. They also have one of the toughest SOBs to ever play quarterback, the late Steve McNair, may God rest his soul. Now that was a real tragedy. McNair was one of those guys you would hit and hit and hit, and he'd just smile like nothing was wrong. I mean, he played with some brutal injuries. He finished up his career with Baltimore, and I wish I had played a few years with that guy. Not only could he throw it, but he could run the length of the field if you let him out of the pocket.

So, like I said, this is a huge game. Tennessee is in a short-yardage play, like third-and-1 or something. They run the play right into the middle, I shoot the gap, and the fullback comes up to lead the way into the hole. Well, this dude has to go through me first. He hits me, and suddenly I can't feel anything. I can't move. I'm freaking paralyzed and freaked out of my mind. I think somebody is lying on top of me because I can't move. The trainer, Bill Tessendorf, runs out to check on me, and I'm yelling at him to get this guy off me. He says, "Goose, there's nobody on top of you." Now this is getting really scary. Tessendorf is doing everything he can to get me to relax. I'm lying on the field, unable to move or turn myself over. This has never happened to me. I've had knee injuries and all sorts of other shit, but this is the first time I've been paralyzed, even temporarily. The worst that's ever happened like that before was having a "stinger" or two. That's where you get a shooting, hot pain from the top of your shoulder through your arm because you got hit a certain way. Guys get that crap all the time. So anyway, I'm lying on the field, and all of a sudden I hear the fans start clapping, cheering, and laughing. I'm paralyzed and they're laughing. Why? Well, I can thank me and my big, storytelling mouth. They think that this is my big signal to Tessendorf that I just crapped my pants, the "I shit myself" signal. I'm sure there are still fans out there who are convinced that the hit meant nothing and I just have a weak sphincter. What can you do except laugh about it now?

This is the scariest thing that has ever happened to me, and all I'm thinking is about how my wife and my mom aren't here. They're watching on TV, and they can't find out what's going on. My brother Elio is in the stands, and he runs down and gets on the field. They put me on this board, and then get me on a stretcher and wheel me off. Literally, I'm crying because I'm so scared at this moment. I'm thinking to myself, *Jesus Christ, I'm paralyzed, how am I going to go through the rest of my life like this? This is crazy.* But then, thankfully, I start to get a little tingle in my fingers. By this time, the place is pretty silent because it's looking a little more serious. But as they wheel me off the field and down the tunnel, this guy shouts out, "He's all right, he just shit his pants." By this time, my hand is better, so I flip that guy the bird.

So they get me back in the locker room, and they're about to cut my pants off to examine me. I say right then, "Listen, don't cut my pants because I've got to go back out there." The doctor says, "No way, we're not clearing you to play." I'm like, "What do you have to do to clear me?" By this time, I'm starting to get the feeling back in my legs, and I say to them, "You have to clear me because if I don't go back out there, I'll never go back on the field again." That's how scared I am. So they get a police escort, get an ambulance, take me to the hospital, stick me in an MRI machine to make sure nothing is structurally wrong, and then hustle me back to the stadium. By the time I get back to the stadium, I can run a little bit, basically jog, and I come back like four plays before the first half is over.

Now, if I was to be in that situation again, I wouldn't go out there. And let me advise young guys: don't do it. The doctors were telling me that after that kind of injury, you're more susceptible to another injury like it, and the next time it could be real paralysis. My brother was looking at me, saying, "Don't go out there, don't go." But at the time, I was just flipped out. I felt like I had to go out there and play. It's like the old saying: I felt like if I didn't get back up on that horse, I was never going to ride again. I think I might have been too scared. As it was, my arms were really weak, I could barely use them. It was like my body was one big funny bone that had just got hit and everything was tingling. But I was going back out there to face Bruce Matthews.

I remember after the game, after I got checked out again by the doctors, I went home, sat in a room alone, and cried because I was so scared. I didn't want to let anybody see that I was crying, so I was just in there by myself. I just completely broke down, saying, "Oh God, I can't believe that I almost was paralyzed." You go through something like that, and all of a sudden all these thoughts go through your head. I was thinking about my kids. It was a crazy moment. Those are the moments that people don't ever see or hear about.

Let's put that into some perspective. Here I am, on the verge of the greatest moment of my career—the Super Bowl run we made in 2000. Of course, I don't really know it at the time, but I know we have a good team. We're in playoff contention, and that's only happened twice in my first ten years. This is big stuff for me. In the midst of all that, I'm facing serious issues about my mortality, like, should I even do this again?

People see us on Sundays and, win or lose, they're entertained. That's what sports is all about: it's a chance to get away from all your problems during the week. Say you're some guy, maybe a plumber or whatever, and you've been dealing with crap all week. Real crap if you're a plumber. You're working hard, sweating your balls off every day to make ends meet. On Sunday you want some release from all the pressure. Either you're going to the game to eat some food, drink a few beers, and yell your head off for three hours, or you're sitting at home and doing pretty much the same thing. We, the football players, get it. We know that we're your outlet on Sunday. No problem, we're playing a game we love, you're paying us to play hard—it's all good for everybody.

But even though we're making a lot of money, it ain't always easy to do this crap. There are moments when you're in life-threatening pain if you play football. Trust me—cops, soldiers, and firemen face a lot worse. They put their lives on the line every day, and we all have serious respect for that. But that doesn't mean it's all rosy as a football player. You can play this game only for so long, and it can literally end at any moment. I was lucky because I got to decide when I was done. After twelve years, I walked away when I knew my body couldn't take it anymore. But I also know how close I came to being toast on that day in Baltimore, playing against Tennessee.

If you play football for a living, you better love it, because the money ain't enough if you don't. There are probably only a handful of guys in the league at any time who can play on talent alone and not on desire. Trust me on that. On days like that one for me, when I was scared out of my mind, there was no amount of money that could have overcome that feeling. There was no amount you could pay me that would have allowed me to say, "Okay, if I end up paralyzed, it's okay." To me, this was more about all the things I had to overcome to be the player I wanted to be, to have all those dreams I had when I was a little kid and wasn't allowed to play because I weighed too much. This was about proving my youth coach wrong, about overcoming two blown-out knees, about sticking it up Mike Gottfried's ass, about proving to all those guys at the Colts why they were wrong to pay me nothing. It was about hearing the Colts' team doctor say that I would maybe play a couple of years and thinking to myself, *To hell with you, doc.* This was about honoring my family and friends at home. Yeah, the money is great, but you need a lot more than that to drive you past possibly being paralyzed.

To me, that's what the 2000 season was about. It was me getting pushed to the limits of what I could handle. It was our whole team getting pushed to the limits of what we could handle, especially from the mental perspective. We had a lot to overcome, collectively and individually. And it started from basically the first minute of the entire year, right after the Super Bowl when St. Louis beat Tennessee and Ray Lewis got in trouble. I mean, talk about a kick in the balls kind of thing. We spent the whole off-season wondering what the hell was going to happen to Ray. It was a freaking circus.

Before I get too deep into the whole thing with Ray, let me explain what Ray means to me. Up until the year I got to Baltimore, I never talked to Ray. I didn't know him at all. He was a first-round pick in 1996, and everybody talked about how good he was, but I didn't pay much attention. After I signed that off-season and showed up in Baltimore, I came in and met him for the first time. Ray came up to me, and I just said, "Hey, what's going on?" He was really jacked up to see me, genuinely happy, and said, "Goose, I'm going to the Pro Bowl because we have you now." He hadn't made the Pro Bowl his rookie year, and that bugged him. Ray wants to be great—you just feel that as soon as you meet him. He looked at me as a guy who could help him, and that was a great feeling for me, that this kid respected me that much before we had ever even played together. He was counting on me to help him. To me, that was more pressure, but I love the pressure. Load it up and let's go. That's what I respond to.

Of course, our first year together he made it to the Pro Bowl, and you could see how much that made him feel good about himself. Look, I'm not taking credit for his career, but it feels great to help somebody like that achieve what he wants and, most importantly, what he's capable of. That's how you develop that trust, that family atmosphere. Ray made it every year we played together in Baltimore, and he won his first Defensive Player of the Year Award in 2000, the year all hell broke loose after the Super Bowl. Think about how determined this guy had to be to come back after sitting in a jail cell for more than a month.

If you don't remember, right after the Super Bowl that year between St. Louis and Tennessee, Ray was out on the streets with some of his friends when a fight broke out with these two guys, Jacinth Baker and Richard Lollar. During the fight, a couple of Ray's friends supposedly stabbed these two guys, and they bled to death right there on the street. In the aftermath, Ray supposedly dumped the clothes he was wearing, and when the police eventually talked to him, he gave them some misleading statements. Ray ended up in jail for a few weeks after that and he and his friends later went on trial, even though Ray never had anything to do with killing those guys. Ray finally had the murder charge dropped, but he had to plead guilty to obstruction of justice. He was given a year of probation and was fined $250,000 by the NFL. It was crazy.

When it happened, I had been in Atlanta for the Super Bowl. My first reaction was to call Kevin Byrne, the Ravens vice president of public relations, and just ask what I could do to help. But there's not really much you can do when the police are already involved. I knew Ray had been in town because I ran into him in Atlanta. Up to then, I don't know if he kept the best company. I had been down in Miami when I got recruited for college, so I get it. If you're from Miami, you have all sorts of people hanging on you. The place is wild. Not that all colleges aren't wild, it's just that Miami has this extra layer of people around the program all the time. The one thing about Ray is, he's not a dumb kid. He's really smart, and I knew he wasn't going to be the guy to put himself in that situation and jeopardize the life he had ahead of him. No way. Now, some of the people around him, they probably didn't give a damn about Ray. It's that whole reflected glory thing—when you're an athlete or somebody prominent, you have people hang around you just because they want to be known as one of your people. When you're an athlete, you have to learn to see through that. You gotta know which people are there because they really care about you and not just about themselves. Everybody wants to have a good time, we get it, but you have to keep it under control.

From that perspective, I think this whole incident really changed Ray for the better. I know it sucked; it was sad for a lot of people. Two guys die, and everybody thinks you somehow had something to do with it, when that's the last thing you'd ever want to do . . . that's gotta hurt. You sit in jail and realize that it can all get taken away in a second, and by things you have no control over. For me, that moment came from getting paralyzed temporarily. For Ray, it was sitting in jail, wearing that orange jumpsuit, and being handcuffed. I know that changed him. When he got back to us when it was all over, after he worked out a plea deal, you just saw this different level of intensity in him. Trust me, Ray was plenty intense before that. But now he had this look like he wasn't going to let anything get in the way of him doing everything he possibly could. I never sat down and talked to Ray about it, but that's because I didn't have to. I could just tell from watching him work. I could tell because I think he really started to understand that the guys he had around him with the Ravens were the guys he could really trust, the guys who weren't just around him to suck up to him.

Now, a lot of that didn't happen right away. Since he was in jail, we didn't see a lot of Ray. He was pretty much shut down. We would ask Byrne if he was all right, and Kevin would give us just enough to make sure we knew he was okay. We had an off-season minicamp, and that was a media circus, even though he wasn't around. We had reporters trying to find out all sorts of stuff about Ray. When they couldn't find out about Ray, they wanted to get inside our heads. What were we supposed to say? We weren't there, we didn't know anything. All we knew was that we cared about Ray, he was our teammate, and we needed him to accomplish what we wanted to do that season. It ain't any more complicated than that. When he finally got back to the team, the media was all over him the entire season. It was crazy. He handled it the best way he could, though: he played his ass off.

As for me, this was the year I finally expected to get paid. When I first signed with Baltimore—when Ted Marchibroda was the coach—we'd made a deal with each other, and Ozzie Newsome knew it. I had to sign a four- or five-year deal to make the numbers work under the salary cap. It was all just pushing the numbers around. Anyway, I told Teddy, "Look, after three years, you have to redo my contract." I wasn't going to be the lowest-paid veteran defensive lineman in the league again. Not after ten years in the NFL. I told Teddy there was no way they were going to do that to me.

So the off-season goes by, and they don't redo the deal. Yeah, they fire Teddy, but that isn't my problem. I'm not going to play unless they pay me. End of story.

We get to the start of training camp, and still no deal. Fine, I'm staying home. Now I've got Rex Ryan, my defensive line coach, and Jack Del Rio, another defensive coach, calling me like every day: "Come on, Goose, we need you. You know you want to play." Okay, you fuckers need me? Pay me. Billick is talking his noise and everything, but I've never been afraid to tell those guys exactly what I want. I love Rex and Jack, but a deal is a deal. Those two start talking some shit too, like about how they're going to drive to my house and kidnap me. Yeah, I'd like to see you guys try.

I finally came back at the end of training camp after a slight adjustment on my contract, and frankly, it was the best thing for me. Instead of being all worn out from getting smacked around in the heat, my body was fresh at the beginning of the season.

Of course, Rex got his revenge. That season we opened up against the Steelers. Even when the Steelers are not very good, they still want to hit the shit out of you. The Steelers and the Ravens play the same style game—it ain't like any other game, it's more like some tribal war. If you've ever seen those shows about how the Samoans and Tongans play rugby, it's like that: an all-out battle for honor.

So we open with Pittsburgh at old Three Rivers Stadium, which is just a shithole with that old, hard Astroturf surface. It's a 1:00 P.M. game, so it's still pretty hot, but Rex has been telling me all week, "Look, I just need you for like sixteen plays." I'm figuring I'll play on first down the whole game, we'll get up on them, and I can rest in the second half. Well, the first quarter ends, and I'm already at like fourteen or fifteen plays. I look over at Rex and give him that look like, *When am I coming out?* He screams back at me, "I meant sixteen plays a quarter."

That asshole. You have to love Rex. What a great coach. To this day, I still think the Ravens should have hired him to be their next head coach. I even told that to Steve Bisciotti, the Baltimore owner, when they hired John Harbaugh. Nothing against Harbaugh, but here was a team that won on defense and had a defensive guy who was great with the players. What else did you need? Bisciotti said, "Rex is a little too close to the guys." Too close? That's the point: you want a coach the players believe in, someone they trust and want to go to war for.

Rex basically taught us to police ourselves. Really, he was a great psychologist. I think he learned just as much from us as we did from him. He'd look at us and say, "You guys know this. You mean I got to show you what you did wrong? You know what you did wrong." He would have us correct ourselves. The other thing Rex did is, he didn't get hung up on the little crap that so many coaches worry about. He'd say, "Get it done. I don't care what you do. Go out, drink, get drunk, do whatever you gotta do during the week. But show up on Sunday, play like hell, and get your job done." And we did. Of course, by that time we had been together for a long time. Well, all of us except Sam Adams.

Sam Adams, now there's a trip. Hall of Fame talent, but he was as out there as you can get. He was a handful, constantly stirring crap. You never knew what you were going to get with Sam, but that was okay because we knew how to handle him. If Sam didn't play hard, we'd tell him right away: get off the field. We'd play Larry Webster in a heartbeat if Sam was a pain in the ass. Sam would see that, and he'd straighten up again for a while.

Sam was a first-round pick and one of the most talented guys you'll ever see—amazing quickness for a man that size. People will tell you that the key to our defense was me and Sam having our best years that season. I don't know about me; I thought I was pretty consistent most of my career. But I can tell you that Sam played hard. He was hard to manage, but he played harder than he had ever played before because we were able to drag what we called his "tri-polar" attitude along with us. That meeting room full of defensive linemen forced it out of him because we stood up to his crap.

It wasn't just that Sam would check out from time to time; he was nasty. He'd make jokes about guys that really were inappropriate. Now, I'm an unfiltered guy, and I say the wrong thing a lot of the time, but I'm never trying to be mean. Sam was a mean-spirited asshole to guys. He would make fun of a guy's mother or wife, but he would do it in a very specific, very nasty way. It wasn't a goofy "yo' mama" joke; it was a reference to something very specific.

Sam was always acting superior to guys because he was so talented and, in the process, would be really demeaning. I think just about every guy in that room wanted to kill Sam at one point or another. Him and Rob Burnett, they got into it one time. We told Rex to leave the room because we knew we had to take care of it among ourselves. So Rob and Sam go at it. Rob throws him up against the wall and puts a giant hole in the drywall. Marvin Lewis is over in the next room talking to the linebackers and the secondary, and he starts yelling through the wall, "What the hell is going on?" We get a big poster and cover up the hole in the drywall. Marvin comes in and asks again what's going on, and we say, "Nothing, just talking." That's how that meeting room was. We fought like crazy in that room, but once we left, we were a band of brothers out on the field. We were tight, even if we had problems.

We also had a blast. One day that season we signed this guy Kelly Gregg to the practice squad. Gregg turned out to be one of the toughest interior linemen in the NFL for a long time. He basically took my job after I retired. But the day he signed, I looked over at him and said, "Who the fuck are you? Better yet, what the fuck are you?" He stood up, put his hand out to shake my hand, and said, "I'm Kelly Gregg, defensive tackle." He was trying to be all polite, but I was just going to bust his balls. He was so young and innocent-looking; he was like a big version of that Buddy Lee doll from the Lee jeans commercial. I was like, "Who got you this job? You had to pull some kind of favor to get here. Hey, guys, look, we signed Buddy Lee." It was all part of the show with the defensive line. If you were going to be in our room, you better have thick skin. Luckily, most of the guys had been around a long time and had been together for a while. Continuity is the secret. If you have guys who trust in each other, you have a foundation to do everything else.

Of course, the other thing people remember most about that season was how shitty our offense was for five weeks. No bones about it, we were awful. We went five consecutive games without a touchdown, and we lost the last three of those. In fact, we were the first team to ever win a Super Bowl after losing three straight games in a season. The first of those losses was the Washington game where I blew the tackle because my stomach was all tied up and I couldn't move. Now remember, before the Washington game we were 5–1, and we had already won back-to-back games without scoring a touchdown. Our kicker, Matt Stover, was saving our ass with four or five field goals. Trust me, no team wants the kicker to be doing that much work. You don't want the kicker to be your hero.

But we were winning, and Tony Banks was our quarterback. Tony was an okay athlete, and he had a pretty big arm, but he just was not very accurate. We didn't need a lot from the quarterback, but we needed something just to get the lead. Then we'd let the defense and our rookie running back, Jamal Lewis (yeah, we had a lot of Lewises that year, including a Jermaine), do the rest of the work to milk the clock. Nice easy formula, except Tony couldn't do it. We got through the Washington game with only three points, and then we got to Tennessee, the game where I got paralyzed. Look, this was a lot to deal with. You start to lose games like this and you get really frustrated. It can tear a team apart. Well, with us, it didn't. We never panicked; we just said, "Okay, let's go, let's beat this team's ass." The next game may have been a tough one, but that was the attitude every time. We never looked beyond that next game. We never thought about what was going to happen the rest of the season with our offense.

The worst thing someone can do is look too far ahead. My wife does that sometimes. She has so many things to do with the kids, running them here, running them there. She starts to look at the whole thing, and she gets overwhelmed. I always say: "It's like painting a picket fence. If you look at the whole fence, you get frustrated. Just pick out the first part and work on that."

I think the big reason we were successful is that we had so many guys who understood how to hang together. There was me and Rob Burnett, a guy who had been with the Ravens when they were in Cleveland and Art Modell ripped them out of that city. If you know about that story, you know how negative that was. The guys on the Ravens who went through that will tell you how much they had to rely on each other to deal with all the negativity.

There was also Ray Lewis having to deal with everything he had gone through. Now, when you put it in perspective, what's five straight games without a touchdown compared to spending a month in jail and almost going to prison? Let's get real. What we were dealing with on the football team was like a problem at preschool compared to that.

Midway through the Tennessee game, as I was dealing with the paralysis, head coach Brian Billick decided to make a switch at quarterback. He brought in Trent Dilfer, the backup, a former starter. Now, Trent wasn't a great quarterback, and he'd had an inconsistent career. But give the guy credit. He came to Baltimore, after being a former first-round pick who failed in Tampa Bay, and just did his job. Yeah, Dilfer could rub some guys the wrong way, but he was tough and he didn't make a lot of mistakes. After he took over, we lost again, this time 9–6 to Pittsburgh—another game without a touchdown. In Baltimore, some radio guy was doing his show from the roof of the station, and he said he wasn't coming down off the roof until the Ravens scored a touchdown. I think that was after the second game. The guy spent like four weeks up on that roof, but it wasn't real funny at the time.

Anyway, after the Pittsburgh game, finally the offense started to take off. The biggest thing was that those guys started to learn each other. Unlike the defense, the guys on offense hadn't played together very much. Dilfer was new, Jamal Lewis was new, and even tight end Shannon Sharpe was new. Sharpe had come over from Denver as a free agent after helping the Broncos win back-to-back Super Bowls. But then Denver started rebuilding and didn't want him back. Okay, fine, we'll take him. Well, as soon as Dilfer got out there, we started really getting the ball to Sharpe a lot more. After the Pittsburgh game, when Sharpe only had three catches,

Dilfer started feeding him. Against Cincinnati, he had seven catches, and we put up 27 points. *Boom,* easy win. He caught eight balls the next week at Tennessee, and we beat the Titans. He caught five passes for 101 yards against Dallas, and we shut their ass out, 27–0.

The rest of the regular season we only had one game where we scored less than twenty-four points. You scored twenty-four points with our defense, and it was lights out. We won the last seven games of the regular season and ended up going 12–4. We had four shutouts and set NFL records for fewest points allowed in a sixteen-game season (165) and the fewest rushing yards ever allowed (970). Nobody ran on us because we were so dominant up front. We were paralyzing for an opposing offense.

Ain't that ironic.

GOOSE TALES WITH . . .
ROB BURNETT

Rob Burnett and Tony Siragusa were teammates and roommates during training camp when they played for the Baltimore Ravens. Born in East Orange, approximately twenty miles from Siragusa's hometown in New Jersey, Burnett said he considers Siragusa "like family."

"I guess we have to keep this PG-13-rated, which cuts out about 75 percent of the stories about Goose. Twenty-five percent is still a lot with him, but it's sort of like the difference between Richard Pryor and Bill Cosby. That's my boy. He's one of a kind, all kinds of stories with him. I remember when we were first talking about signing him as a free agent in Baltimore. Marvin Lewis, our defensive coordinator, called me in, and he was looking at film of Goose and asking what I thought. I actually played against Goose when I was at Syracuse, so I knew about him. He had a great reputation, and when you watched the film, you could see why. For being a big old fat guy, he still played from sideline to sideline. He ran to the ball every play, and it's the old saying, you can't teach attitude and hustle. That's a big thing he brought to us that we really needed. We had guys who played hard, but we needed a big guy in the middle who really led the way.

"Goose is right about the defensive line room. It was almost like a steel cage match every week once we got Sam Adams. He was a trip. I love him to death, and he was probably on the best behavior of his career with us because we had a unique group that could handle him. But he was a moody, selfish, self-centered kid. Whatever day it was, you had to ask which Sam you were going to get, and even then he could flip on you in a day. Literally, we'd ask Sam, 'Which guy are we getting today?'

That's why we used to call him 'Sybil' and 'Tri-polar.' Sam would sit in the back of the room by the thermostat and turn it up to like ninety-five degrees. It was hard enough to stay awake as it was, and then it would be so hot in there everybody was falling asleep. The only way we stayed awake was Goose would come in and take off his shoes. It was these shoes he'd worn without socks for like a year. Those stinky feet would keep the whole room awake.

"Out of the eight or nine guys on the defensive line, probably all but one of us got into it with Sam at one time or another. The only guy who didn't was Mike McCrary. He didn't pay Sam any mind, which was probably the way to handle Sam. I didn't pay much attention to him either, but some guys just couldn't handle his sense of humor. Sam was real condescending, real selfish. He'd start making fun of guys, talking about their mothers and stuff, and some guys were real sensitive about that. I know Sam once did that with Rex [Ryan, the defensive line coach at the time], and I could see that Rex wanted to go after him, but Rex took the high road. Rex was great at being able to turn it around on Sam, turn something nasty that Sam said into a joke. Rex could turn something really tense into something warm and fuzzy real quick. He was a master at how he handled the room.

"The one time I got into it with Sam, I knew I had to strike first. Sam has like a hundred pounds on me. Where I was raised, we swing first; you don't want to be on your heels, especially with a guy like that. So I planted him up against the wall, and then the cavalry came in to break it up. But that was the thing about our room that Goose is right about. We had our issues in the room, but we left it in the room. Once we got on the field, we were all together. If somebody tried to take on one of us, he was going to have to deal with eight or nine guys. That's the way it was, and I was never with a group that was that tight any other time in my career.

"On most teams, the defensive line room is usually the most fun room. But our defensive line room will never be replicated in the NFL. With us, when the linebackers and the defensive backs would get done with their meeting, they'd come into our room because we'd usually have food and we were having fun. Goose was the court jester, always saying something funny, and I was the master of superimposing images of people in awkward situations. I'd go through the media guide and get mug shots of everybody and put them in some unique situations. You might see somebody's face in a compromising situation with a farm animal or maybe on some leather-clad, sexually alternative person. Whatever it was, we were having fun. Nothing was off-limits.

"Goose was the guy that basically kept everybody loose. He'd show up to the meetings half-naked with his stinky feet, and then he'd just say whatever. At the time, we had Mike Smith [now the Atlanta Falcons coach] just starting out in the NFL. He was the defensive quality control coach. Really smart guy. He's one of five eventual head coaches we had on that staff. That's amazing. He probably helped cut the preparation time for the coaches in half with all the computer stuff he knew how to do. But back then, if he got four hours of sleep a night, that was a good night. He'd sit in the back of the room, and he'd doze off every once in a while. Goose would start firing spitballs at him to wake his ass up. What you have to know about Goose is that he has the biggest heart in the world. He never means any harm when he says stuff. And that's how he played. He might cut up all week in the meeting room, but then it was all business on Sunday until that final whistle.

"When the game was over and the cameras came out, Goose was

like one of those video machines where you put a quarter in and it won't stop. He was made for the camera, and he's so great at improv. I bet with FOX he's probably one of those guys that get all that stuff in the middle of the week to prepare for the game, and it's all sitting in his office unopened. He doesn't need any of that. But on game day he's giving you 130 percent, and you can see he does that now. It's like when he played—he was a hustler and he loved it. He probably hurt more of our guys by hustling to the ball and running over them than anybody we played against. We all wanted to win: for ourselves, for each other, for Rex, the whole thing.

"We were like family and Goose was right in the middle of that. I remember his first year there, my parents couldn't make it down for Thanksgiving, so I ended up going over to his house with him, Kathy, and Samantha, the only one they had at the time. I felt right at home because he's such a special guy and they're all such real people.

"We hit it off right from the start. The day he signed, we went to Hooters together and just hung out. Certain people you just feel that way about right from the start. We got to the point we were roommates in camp and on the road. He was the only guy I would room with, and I was the only guy he would room with. We were just like that, even if there was a lot to put up with. I've never met a more flatulent, loud-snoring, take-a-dump-with-the-bathroom-door-open guy than Goose. But I love the guy."

THE BIGGEST
GAME

After we got done with the regular season, let's just say our team was confident. Really confident. Look, we had survived a stretch of five consecutive games without scoring a touchdown. We had lost three games in a row. We had changed quarterbacks. We had done all sorts of things. But by the end of the season, we had won seven straight games, including beating archrival Tennessee at its place. Only two of the seven games were decided by less than a touchdown. We were rolling.

So we get to the playoffs and we're feeling like we're big-time. Anyway, as we're getting ready to play our first playoff game, we have a Family Day event. All the wives and kids and everybody are scheduled to come out and celebrate what we're about to do and what we've already done. It's a nice little break—and for the defensive linemen it's a big break.

The day of the party, we're having a light practice, just wearing the basic protective shells and not our full shoulder pads. As we're out at practice, the defensive line is over off to a corner of the field. There's this little wall next to the corner where this little hill goes up to the main building of our training facility. Anyway, Rex has us pushing the buckboard, a single-man blocking sled. On my turn, I push it pretty far back toward the wall. After we push the buckboard, we have to run, so I run down that way around the side of the wall. All of a sudden, I'm around the corner of the building and I see there are like ten cases of beer around the back door, which leads to the kitchen and catering. They've put them out there because there's plenty of snow on the ground and it's cold. So I duck down there, open up a case, and chug a couple of beers. Then I go back up and tell Mike McCrary and Rob Burnett. I'm like, "There's beers down there, and I've got them opened up. Go down and have a few." McCrary goes and gets a couple, then Burnett goes, and then some of the other guys. We must drink something like a whole case during this drill, which goes about twenty minutes.

Now we're all a little drunk, but we keep going. We keep doing drills and grabbing beers and chugging them down. We finish another case, and we're throwing the empties down by the side of the building. Finally, we get to the team portion of practice, the part where we're all supposed to go out there with the first-team defense against the first-team offense. After one play, all of us are tapping out, telling Rex, "We're done, we can't practice anymore." Rex is looking at us like, "What are you guys doing?" What we're doing is trying to enjoy the buzz. He's looking at us and asking, "Are you guys okay?" We're like, "We're good, everything is fine. No problems." Meanwhile, we keep running back to the cases whenever we can. I think we drank just about all ten cases. It was awesome; we were having a great time in practice.

After practice, we had to go do press conferences and interviews with the media. We were drunk off our asses, and we totally blew up the press conference. It was hysterical. But none of it mattered because we always showed up on Sunday and kicked ass.

By the time we got to that point with our defense, we were ridiculous. Like I said, we knew each other so well that we could do just about anything right in the moment. Marvin Lewis, our defensive coordinator, would make some call we didn't like, and we'd change it right on the spot. Marvin would call some weird stunt or something he came up with at that moment, and we'd look at each other and just say something basic. I'd look at Ray Lewis and say, "Under, Cover 2." That's as simple a defense as we had. We didn't have to do too many crazy blitzes or anything. We didn't have to get fancy. We didn't have to outsmart anybody; we just outplayed them. We'd set up in our normal defense, and it was an all-out rush to the quarterback.

See, coaches get it all wrong. They think it's about how many fancy plays they can design, and they want to put more and more in. Really, it's basic stuff that works. The key thing is for players to know what the guy next to them is going to do. Then they can change stuff up from there. They know what's coming, they're just better at doing it. We were the same way in Baltimore. I'd say to McCrary, you shoot inside and I'll cover you. Look, I was at the other end of the spectrum for a long time. I was on a 1–15 team in Indianapolis. Our biggest problem wasn't that we weren't talented; it was that we didn't trust each other. We had guys trying to do somebody else's job, and when that happens, everything falls apart. The key is always to just do your job and keep it simple.

On our defense in Baltimore, we just played one gap. That's where you pick a side of the offensive lineman and just go straight up the field, trying to create havoc along the way. I knew that all I had to do was take care of the A-gap. Somebody else would handle the B-gap. All of a sudden, you're not thinking, you're just reacting and playing. And that's how you play sports. If you ever hear some youth coach during a game say, "You gotta think about what you're doing," that coach doesn't know what he's talking about. You think in practice, but when you play, you just go. The only exception to that is if you're playing next to a guy and you don't know what he's going to do. That's when you start doubting him, start doubting the system, and like I said, everything falls apart.

The year I was in Indianapolis and we almost went to the Super Bowl, we got that far because we formed an incredible trust in each other. By the time we got it revved up in Baltimore, we were even more dominant. That year we were as close to perfect, in terms of that trust and level of execution, as you could ever imagine. I'm not BSing about that. We would go through games with zero breakdowns on defense. When we did review sessions, I think it frustrated the shit out of Marvin because he didn't have anything to say. When you review the tape of the previous game, it usually takes like three hours for most teams in most seasons. You're talking about a missed assignment here, or what went on over there. It takes forever sometimes. That season in Baltimore, our review sessions would sometimes be twenty minutes. Seriously, twenty, maybe thirty minutes tops, because everybody was perfect. Even during the twenty or thirty minutes, Marvin had to come up with something, so he'd nitpick about the littlest shit.

Everyone just did their job, and did it unbelievably, no breakdown. We'd just sit there with the tape running, and it wouldn't stop. On to the next play, fine. On to the next play, perfect. On to the next play, great.

That's when we knew we were really good, and that's what we were like as we were going into the playoffs.

We opened the playoffs on New Year's Eve against Denver at home. This was the Broncos a couple of years after John Elway retired and after running back Terrell Davis got hurt. This team had Gus Frerotte at quarterback, Mike Anderson at running back, and they still had that bullshit, chop-blocking offensive line coached by Alex Gibbs and head coach Mike Shanahan running the whole team. All you'd ever hear from other defensive linemen around the league was how dirty the Broncos were, especially after Denver ran for like two hundred yards or some shit like that. Not against us. They rushed for forty-two yards in that game, and we sacked Frerotte four times, knocking him out of the game. The best part of the game was when Shannon Sharpe, who had just played for Denver on its two championship teams, scored a fifty-eight-yard touchdown, giving us a 14–3 lead in the second quarter. That's all we needed. The Broncos didn't get two hundred yards of total offense against us as we beat them, 21–3.

The next game was a huge one. We had to go back to Tennessee and play the Titans for the third time that season. The first time we played them was right in the middle of the season, when we went through that five-game stretch without a touchdown. They beat us 14–6, so it wasn't like they blew us out. The next time, we went to their place and beat them, 24–23. They ended up winning the division with a 13–3 record, and since we were 12–4, now we had to go on the road again. Until we beat them earlier that season, they had never lost in their home stadium. (Then again, they had only played there for like three years.) But as I said before, they were big and tough with a lot of good players like Steve McNair at quarterback and Eddie George at running back.

Now, if you measure stats, we shouldn't have won this game. Not even close. We finished the game with 134 yards of total offense. We had two punts blocked. It's hard enough to win when you get one punt blocked, let alone two, but the fact is that we ended up basically blowing them out, 24–10, in their place. I know that ain't 40–0 or anything like that, but this was like domination. That's because our special teams came up with two huge plays, blocking two field goals. The second one was returned ninety yards by Anthony Mitchell in the fourth quarter. Then Ray Lewis intercepted a pass and returned it fifty yards for a touchdown. That all came after Sharpe had another long touchdown, another fifty-eight-yarder. But this is what you should know: we allowed a touchdown on the first drive of the game. George scored on a two-yard run. As it turned out, that was the only touchdown our defense allowed the entire playoffs. That's it, one score. In fact, our defense scored more touchdowns. That's how dominant we were over a four-game stretch.

The next stop was Oakland, where I got to be reunited with my man Al "Every day is a new day" Davis. It might have been years later, but I wasn't going to forget that shit. Anyway, the Raiders were doing their usual badass routine, acting like they were the roughest, toughest team in the history of the league. That was all that Davis attitude, which he tried to rub off on the players and the fans. You had all the fans in their outfits and face paint—it was a freak show. They were all jacked up at the start of the game, but by the end it was like we stole their lunch money and kicked their asses. Trust me when I say this game was special, really special. We beat them 16–3, and they never had a chance. It was a phenomenal ass-whipping, right down to my hit on Oakland quarterback Rich Gannon.

Now, remember when I said that our defense had basically become a race to the quarterback by this point in the season? Trust me when I say it was like that. I'm not just talking shit. During our four playoff games, we had fourteen sacks, including six from McCrary, which is unreal. To put that in perspective, it's hard to get fourteen sacks in the regular season against shitty teams. We were doing that against the best the NFL had to offer. McCrary was on fire. It was brutality at its finest. The other teams were so freaked out about who to block that they made mistake after mistake.

That's where I come in with Gannon, getting the biggest hit of my life. Early in the second quarter, it's a first-and-10 situation, but we know they're a pass-heavy team. Shit, Jon Gruden is coaching them, and all he ever wants to do is throw. So we're ready to pass-rush. As soon as the ball is snapped, we have McCrary run inside of me. He starts off on my right and then runs in front of me to the left, toward the middle of the field. As soon as he does that, the Raiders leave me unblocked. Completely unblocked. By the time I get to Gannon, I have a seven-yard head start and I'm at full speed. I may be 342 pounds, but I'm damn quick, and it's not like I can all of a sudden just stop. As I get to Gannon, he's releasing the ball and I just plant him. It's one of those great hits where you get every ounce of your body into it. As he falls, I can hear the air go completely out of his body. I just crush him. It's a clean shot—hard, but not dirty. Yeah, I give him every pound I can, but that's what I'm supposed to do.

Of course, not everybody sees it that way. The Oakland players and fans are all crying because I've just laid Gannon out. He's crumpled on the field, complaining about his shoulder. Shit, all he had was a bruised shoulder. Worse, the broadcasters on CBS, freaking Phil Simms and the play-by-play guy, Greg Gumbel, start complaining on air about me. Of course, Simms is a former quarterback. He was one of my dad's favorites because he played for the Giants. He was a tough guy. At least I thought he was. Right on national TV he starts saying, "That is illegal, that is absolutely illegal." These freaking quarterbacks stick together like little old ladies playing bridge and having tea.

Look, that's how you play. The Raiders had to bring in Bobby Hoying. You could just see that the Raiders were mentally done by then—not that they had much chance before that. We had already intercepted Gannon once in the first quarter. Gannon tried to come back in the second half, but he was in too much pain. Meanwhile, we ended up with four interceptions and we got another big play from Sharpe. This time Dilfer hit him on a quick slant for ninety-six yards. The play came on third-and-18—it was completely crazy. That shit should never happen to a great defense. We got that play and three field goals, and it was lights out. The Raiders never had a chance. We won 16–3, but it might as well have been 50–0; that's how much of a chance the Raiders had. They finished the game with seventeen yards rushing. That ain't a misprint. They had seventeen yards on the ground. They couldn't move the ball more than a couple of inches at a time.

So we get home and all of a sudden I'm hearing about how the NFL might fine me for my hit on Gannon. What's this bullshit? The refs didn't throw a flag or anything like that—it was a clean hit—but as the NFL usually does, touch a quarterback too hard and they fine you. When I get called about this by the league office, I'm actually back in New Jersey driving around because we have extra time before the Super Bowl. Here I am on the way to the Super Bowl for the first time, and I have to take this call about how the league is going to fine me $10,000 for a clean hit. What a bunch of crap. So I'm on the side of the road in New Jersey on this conference call with my agent and this guy from the NFL. I listen to him say that I should have been able to hold up and not put all my weight on him. I'm like, "Dude, have you seen me? I'm kind of a big dude. Once I get started, it's not that easy to stop." The NFL guy keeps reading me the rules and talking about holding up on the hit and all this other shit. I'm like, "Dude, you go ahead and fine me because that's what you want to do, but that's fucking bullshit and you know it." My agent calls me back after the call and says, "Well, it looks like we lost that one. Way to go."

Whatever, I didn't give a shit. Like I said back then, it didn't matter. If it had cost me $20,000, or even more, I would have paid it to go to the Super Bowl, not that I was going to tell them that.

But here's the best part. For those next couple of days, they have Gannon on ESPN and all that. He's talking about how hurt he is and all this crap. Well, I'm lying in bed with my wife as we're watching TV, and she comes up with the best line. Now, you have to know first that my wife is all of about five-foot-one and one hundred pounds. So she hears Gannon complaining and says, "You jump on me twice a week, and I don't complain about it. If I complain, do I get $10,000?" That was a gem, just beautiful. So I go back to Baltimore and tell the media guys what my wife said. They're all cracking up. What can Gannon say in response to that?

Anyway, after a week back in Baltimore, it was on to Tampa Bay and Super Bowl week. What a great week. We had the whole Ray Lewis drama to deal with again, but we had been through that about a thousand times already. There wasn't a question they could ask any of us, even Ray, that we couldn't deal with. We had our coach, Brian Billick, talking all kinds of shit about how we were going to come in like screaming banshees, or whatever the hell he was saying. But look, Brian was good to us in a lot of ways. The whole week at the Super Bowl, we didn't have a curfew. He made a point to tell us that he was going to let us be men, that he didn't think it was right to knock on a man's door at night to make sure he was there. I appreciated that, because we knew how to take care of business. We didn't have guys doing stupid shit. We had guys who were there to win. We might have been talking shit, but we knew we could back it up, and we always brought it on game day. Plus, Billick promised me that I might get the ball on offense. We had to be up by four touchdowns, but I had a chance. That said, Brian got to be a little full of himself after a while. It's like all these coaches think they have this amazing ability to control people or whatever. Look, you organize a team, you get guys to play for you, you get good players, but other than that, you stay out of the way. Head coaches are really facilitators; they're not really coaches anymore.

That's what I always believe is the key thing for coaches. That's why you see Rex Ryan having so much success the first two years on the job. He comes to a new team that's completely a mess, has a young quarterback, and takes them to back-to-back AFC Championship Games. That's because Rex doesn't pretend he has all the answers. He trusts his players, he talks to them and brings them in. It's like when I was talking to someone from Baltimore about Rex. This person told me they weren't going to hire Rex as the head coach because Rex was "too close to the players." What is that? That's what you want with a football team. This isn't a corporation, this is a football team. Give me a bunch of guys who love me, trust me, and will go and kill for me and I'll show you a fucking army. Show me a hundred guys who don't know me, don't know what I'm about, and don't trust me and I'll show you a team that can't win.

Rex can go into a meeting room, and he'll say: "Listen, you guys have nothing to worry about. The media will come after me, they'll make fun of me, they'll write about me. I'll give them shit to write about. You guys worry about playing football. I'll take care of everything else. If you get in trouble, I'll tell them I was there." I had a defensive line coach back in Indianapolis named Greg Blache, one of the smartest coaches I have ever had. The year before we went to the AFC Championship Game, he said to us, "You guys went and sacrificed everything for me and my family, you paid my bills. If any of you guys ever murder somebody, you call me and I'll go on the witness stand and tell them you were with me." That's how I grew up. I appreciated that. If Greg Blache called me up right now, I'd be there for him. If Rex called me up and said, "Goose, I need this," I would say, "No problem."

So we get to Super Bowl week, and who else would we be playing but the New York Giants, my dad's team. It had been more than eleven years since he passed away, but here I was facing his team in the biggest game of my life. The Giants had an all-right team. I remember, leading up to the game, Mike Strahan of the Giants and I posed for the cover of *Sports Illustrated* for a preview of the game. I work with Mike now on FOX, but this game wasn't going to be close. No how, no way. I wasn't the only one who was confident, but I was out there. And I wasn't afraid to put myself out there.

The night before the Super Bowl, my buddy Eddie Toner comes down for the game, and some friends of mine have an RV that they and my family are going to use for tailgating the next day. Well, it's the night before the game, and I can't sleep. I want to see what's going on around town. We don't have a curfew or anything because Billick wouldn't do it. So I tell Toner, "Let's go out." He's looking at me like I'm crazy. Whatever, the game isn't until the next night. What am I supposed to do, be a hermit or something and stay in? I want to see if the town is getting excited for the game. Toner is like, "Tony, it's the Super Bowl, I think the town is pretty excited." Whatever, I'm going out.

So we get in the RV and head over to Ybor City, which is where a bunch of the bars and clubs are, and it's great. The best part is that I find a hot dog cart that has corn dogs, cheese dogs, and chili dogs. I have one of each. Toner is looking at me like, "That's disgusting, what are you eating the night before the Super Bowl?" Toner doesn't understand—those hot dog carts are where you find the best food. It's like 11:00 P.M. and I need a good snack.

On the day of the game, I show up at the stadium about five or six hours before the rest of the team. I find some game programs, you know, the fancy magazine they sell on game day for the fans. Well, I get enough for every player on the team, and I find the page with the picture of all the different Super Bowl rings that all the previous winners have gotten.

I never told anybody what I did next, although the trainers helped me. I cut out that page from every program and put it in front of every player's locker so that when they walk in, all they're going to see are Super Bowl rings. I want every player to be reminded one last time: this is what we're going for, and we have to fucking get this thing. The intensity is so deep in me that day, but this is what you work your whole life for. This is the payoff. This is what so many people work so hard to help you get. This is what you do to prove all the doubters wrong: from my youth coach Bill Chango, to Frank D'Alonzo, to the Colts team doctor, to Ron Meyer, and to whoever else I ran into along the way. This is what makes it worth it to fight through the fear of being paralyzed. This is what makes up for sitting around for two days waiting to get drafted and having nobody take you. This is what makes up for crying after you didn't get picked for the all-star team.

The craziest part of the Super Bowl isn't even really the game. It's controlling your adrenaline in those moments right before the game starts. Of course, there's some funny stuff. As we're lining up in the tunnel, looking around, there's this one guy up there, a Giants fan, with what looks like his three-year-old son up on his shoulders. It should be this sort of cool sight, but the kid has both his hands up, giving us the double bird. Safety Rod Woodson, one of our Hall of Fame guys, turns to me and says, "Look, another future doctor."

Anyway, as I'm waiting in the tunnel, I'm totally tuned in to the announcer's voice. The crowd is so loud, you're just doing everything you can to concentrate on the announcer. The last thing you want is to have the announcer call your name and you don't run onto the field. As I'm standing there, this guy is holding me back. He pushes me back twice. I think if he had pushed me one more time, I would have killed him. Finally, they call my name, and I run on the field. It's nuts. Even though there are three times as many Giants fans as Baltimore fans in the place (come on, it's the Giants, one of the oldest teams in the league), you can totally hear the Ravens fans. It isn't like playing a road game or something like that. We get out on the field, and it's crazy, so much more than a regular game. Ray comes out and does his funky pregame dance. You can feel a year's worth of frustration and anger pouring out of Ray that whole game. He was on a mission that whole year, but never more than on that day. The halftime show has *NSYNC, Aerosmith, Britney Spears, Nelly, and Mary J. Blige. The national anthem is sung by Ray Charles. How much more over the top can you get? Trying to explain this is like telling somebody who has never had kids what it's like to be a father. You can't explain it all. Until you actually do it, you have no idea.

The game starts, and it's pretty typical for us. We're trading possessions with the Giants for most of the first quarter (the first five possessions end in punts) before we finally get a little break and Jermaine Lewis returns a punt into Giants territory. This is where Dilfer comes through with a big thirty-eight-yard throw to Brandon Stokley for our first touchdown. Like I said before, Dilfer didn't have to do a lot, but he had to come up with a play or two every game. That's exactly what happened. In the first three games, he had big TD passes to Sharpe. This time he gets it to Stokley, a great story himself. Stokley had been a fourth-round pick the year before, caught one ball as a rookie, eleven more in 2000, and suddenly he's scoring the first touchdown for us against the New York Giants and he's doing it against Jason Sehorn, who the media is pumping up as some great player.

Dilfer, Stokley, and the rest of the offense have been working on setting up that play for the whole week leading up to the game. They know that Sehorn can be had, because Sehorn can't turn and run fast enough. His makeup speed just isn't very good. So here we are, taking a shot at one of their big-time name players, and all of a sudden you can see that the Giants are a little unraveled. Plus, they're really frustrated by this time. On our previous possession, Giants linebacker Jessie Armstead intercepted a pass and returned it for a touchdown, but the play got called back by a penalty on the Giants.

Basically, the Giants were reeling by this time. We got a field goal in the second quarter and then really took control in the third quarter when Duane Starks returned an interception for a touchdown. Then we exchanged kickoff return touchdowns. That was New York's only score, a kickoff return because one guy missed a tackle. We were that close to getting the first shutout in Super Bowl history. The Giants had sixteen possessions, all of them ended with a turnover, a punt, or the clock running out. We held them to 152 total yards of offense and got five turnovers and four sacks. It was the third-fewest yards any team had ever allowed. It was total dominance from start to finish. At the end of the game, they kept telling me to get off the field, basically take a congratulatory walk to the sideline. I was like: "Fuck no, fuck that, no way, they ain't fucking scoring on us. I ain't letting this motherfucker go. I'm waiting for the fat lady to sing before I get off the fucking field."

You want to know how intense we were on defense? On the Giants' final four possessions of the game, they didn't even cross midfield. You should have seen the look in their eyes by the end of the game. I'm not going to say they were scared, but they were totally demoralized. It was like we just said to them, "You're not going anywhere unless we let you go there." Ray Lewis was named the most valuable player of the game. Of course, the Disney people weren't going to have Ray do the "I'm going to Disneyland!" line for the commercial, so Dilfer did it. The only guys who get to do that line now are the winning quarterbacks, which is BS if you ask me.

But that's what the game is all about, catering to the quarterbacks and the offensive guys. Here's a little stat that proves my point: there have been forty-six Super Bowls, and the MVP has been a defensive guy all of eight times. Seriously, *eight.* Quarterbacks? Twenty-five times one of those pretty boys has been the MVP. Look, I get the fact that the quarterback is important, but this stuff has gotten out of whack.

Whatever, the fact that Ray got the MVP was a big moment for our entire defense after the year we had. I know it was important for Ray too. That was redemption for him, and it was part of learning that changing his life around was really important. You look at Ray today and he has become such a great leader. The thing I'm so proud of with him is that he has carried our tradition of great defense on for a decade. The Ravens are still a defense-first team. That tradition started with our group playing our asses off for an entire season.

I can't begin to tell you how much that game meant to me. My whole life was transformed by that game, it literally created and gave me a springboard to the life I have now. I don't care what anybody says, the Super Bowl is not just another game. If you lose that game, you can say it was a great season, but you know it really felt like it sucked because only one team gets to walk away feeling like a winner. You can talk to me all you want about how great the Buffalo Bills were in those four straight seasons they lost the Super Bowl . . . bullshit, I know those guys felt like it sucked. It's not the same thing as when you win. It's not even close.

That's the biggest game you will ever be in. I've met guys who made the Hall of Fame or played in the Pro Bowl umpteen times. If they can't walk around with a Super Bowl ring on, it sucks. If you have that ring that says WORLD CHAMPIONS, earned playing the most violent, testosterone-packed game in the world, it's an amazing feeling. When you win that game, your dick gets bigger. If you have a one-inch dick and you win that game, now it's two inches. You can be the ugliest motherfucker in the history of the world, but if you win that game, you'll marry one of the hottest women ever. When I even just let friends of mine try on my Super Bowl ring, they get tingles down below.

Just look at Tom Brady. His cock is probably two feet long and he married a supermodel, that's a fact. Well, the second part is a fact. Hell, his wife is such a big-time supermodel, she makes more money than he does. Need I say more?

GOOSE TALES WITH . . .
REX RYAN

Before becoming the ever-quotable coach of the New York Jets, Rex Ryan was an assistant coach with the Baltimore Ravens. Ryan started off as the defensive line coach before finishing up as the defensive coordinator. Along the way, he coached Tony Siragusa. These days the two live only a few miles apart in New Jersey and remain close friends.

"You have to know that underneath all of Goose's big talk is a softie, a really good guy. I have a million stories I could tell you about working with him, but I'll keep it to a couple of my favorites. The year we played the AFC Championship Game at Oakland and then won the Super Bowl, sometime before the game we're all sitting around BSing. So I'm getting the guys revved up, asking each of them what they're going to do with all the playoff money after we win. It's not that you win so much as it's like you get this pretty sweet bonus on top of the fact that you're in the playoffs and how exciting that is. Anyway, it gets back to me, and I start to talk about how I'm going to finish out my basement, get a big-screen TV and all that kind of stuff, maybe buy my wife a van. So we go play that game, and Goose goes, 'I have your TV.' He said it while we were on the plane flying back to Baltimore. I look at him and say, 'Bullshit, no, don't do that.' He just repeats it and says, 'No, I got the TV.'

"We go to the Super Bowl, kick ass on the New York Giants, and now I'm back at home in Baltimore finishing out the basement in the winter. One day, here it comes: Goose has two of his buddies with him, and he has this huge-ass TV in the back of this pickup. I'm like, 'Goose, come on, man. You don't need to do that.' He's like, 'Bullshit.' I tell him to at least let me pay for half of it. Again, he says, no way. I ask him where he got it, and he says, 'Let's just say it fell off of a truck.' After all these years knowing Goose, you just don't ask. But he's a man of his word. I never knew that before I started working with him. This guy will give you the shirt off his back, and he'll do that for anybody who is close to him, any of his teammates. That's just how he is.

"Here's another perfect example. We were getting ready to play Cincinnati on the day after Christmas in 1999. We had this defensive end named Fernando Smith. He was just with us for that one year. He was kind of a journeyman, and Goose didn't like him all that much, but that didn't matter. On Christmas Eve, Smith is trying to deep-fry a turkey in his apartment, and the thing spills, causing this big grease fire. Luckily, nobody got hurt, but all the presents and all his family's clothes got burned up in the fire. It was just a mess. All the guy has to wear is like some sweatpants and sweatshirts. Everything was gone. He came into our meeting on Christmas Day with a T-shirt and slippers on, it was terrible. The guy had three kids and a wife, just a bad situation for the whole family. Anyway, that day, we're getting ready to go to the team hotel, and Goose comes up to me and says, 'Rex, I'm not going to be at bed check.' I'm like, 'I gotcha, no problem.' I knew he was doing something important, and he helped me enough that I would vouch for him anytime. What I didn't know is, he went home, took presents from underneath his tree, and gave them to Fernando Smith's wife. That's him. Then he went and grabbed like $20,000 of unopened Nike stuff and gave it all to Fernando Smith so the guy would have some clothes. He's just that way, that's him.

"When he was temporarily paralyzed, that was crazy. We were play-ing Tennessee, he collides with the fullback, and they end up carting him off on a stretcher in the first half. Later on, we find out that there's like spinal fluid leaking, some shit like that, but in the second half I look around, and he's standing there right next to me. He went to the hospital, got checked out, and got back on the field. I don't know how the hell he did that. I look at him and say, 'What the fuck are you doing?' He says, 'I'm okay.' His nose is all busted up, and he looks terrible, and I say, 'No, you ain't okay. I'm not letting you in the game.' He says, 'Nah, the doctor said it's okay, put me in.' Again, I'm like, 'Bullshit, you have to worry about your family.' He looks right back at me and says, 'I'm worried about your family. Put me in the game.' That's who Tony Siragusa is, he's tough and he's loyal. That's what he stands for. When you have guys like that in football, you can do anything.

"With Goose, all I would do with him was say, 'Take away that half of the formation.' He'd step up, take on the guard and the center on his side, and just wipe out anything on his side. He was amazing. People look at him and say, 'He's just some big fat guy.' They have no idea how great an athlete he is. It's not just about toughness, but quickness and strength. When I got to Baltimore, I would make our defensive linemen do up-downs for punishment. It was part punishment and part conditioning. It reminded guys to do stuff the right way, because on an up-down you have to basically fall to the ground and pop back up as fast as possible. It's really tiring, especially for the big defensive linemen. Tony never had a problem. He could grind out forty up-downs like it was nothing, like he was some little cornerback or something. Man, was he an awesome player."

1|2

FAMILY MAN

To see me today, you'd think, "This is the wild and crazy Tony Sira-gusa?" The guy coaching his daughter's soccer team is the same guy who once mooned an NFL team executive? The guy coaching his son's football team is the same guy who threw his roommate's TV out the window in college? Yes, these days I am Mr. Responsibility. I'm juggling a TV career with a wife, three kids, a dog, and all sorts of other things, like running a restaurant. This is how wonderful my life has turned out. But it took a few years of having fun to get here.

That's why I'm careful with my kids. My oldest daughter, she's a beautiful girl. She's in high school and recently started dating. Well, I have rules about dating. The guy has to meet me. So this guy comes to the house, and I bring him into a room with me and a bunch of my buddies. He seems like a nice enough kid, but I have to explain some things. I look him in the eye and I tell him how important my daughter is to me. I tell him, "If something happens that is not right, I don't get mad and I don't get even . . . but my friends here do." Next thing I know, the kid is in the kitchen breathing into a paper bag. My wife Kathy is helping him, and she's not smiling at me. What's the problem? I didn't do nothing.

I listened to Bill Parcells one time, and he talked about the fact that everybody has a button, and it's about finding the button in that person. It can be as simple as saying, "You can't do that." That's what it was for me so many times as a kid, whether it was being an all-star in Little League or being told by Bill Chango that maybe I needed to find some other sport to play besides Pop Warner football. As a coach myself now, I'm the guy who is looking for kids who remind me of myself at that age. I'm not looking for all the stars (although my son is a pretty darn good player right now). Give me the kid who no one thinks can do anything. In particular, I have a soft spot for the kids who are overweight, who nobody wants to work with. I'll find the button to push and I'll make them go.

For me when I was their age, it was about proving that people like Chango were wrong. I never wanted people in the stands to look out there and say in front of my mother or father or brothers, "Oh, that guy can't play, that guy sucks." I always wanted them to have the ammunition to say, "Oh yeah? That guy is going to kick ass," and then I'd go back it up. I never wanted to let them down. It wasn't about me as much as it was about me defending them, representing all they worked for and all they did to support me. Now that I'm a dad, I see the value of getting that out of a kid. Everybody talks about being positive all the time, but that's not it. Look, you're not trying to tell a kid he's a bad person or that he sucks. But sometimes you have to find a way to get him to fight for himself and show him how great it is when he gets that out of himself.

When I'm coaching a kid, all of a sudden I see him go out there and fight his ass off. He may not be the best player on the team, but he's going to go in there and fight and bust his ass every time. I get the biggest charge out of that. The kid might be a wiseass like I was—no problem. The wiseasses are the best, because you can find that button so fast—you know they're motivated by pride. They want to be good, but they just don't have anybody who knows how to handle them. It's like how I used to talk shit to the older kids when I was growing up. They would beat my ass, but I kept coming back for more because I believed in myself. I'd never give up. Beat me up and I'll just run back at you and give you the finger. Now when I coach and I can get a kid to really give everything he has, that moment gives me a little bit of a rush.

The thing is, I've had my share of the party. All that *Jersey Shore* crap you see these days, I did all that. I did that twenty-five years ago. The fighting, the running around, the acting like you're big-time when you're just a punk—all of it. Snooki and all those types, they're not originals. They're just the latest version of all the people I grew up with and even people before that. But I've gone from that to doing lacrosse with my son because that's what's important. I've gone from that to taking my family, including my mom and brothers, back to Italy to see the homeland, to drive the countryside and enjoy everything about it. One time we stopped in the middle of nowhere to look at this beautiful river. Everybody was saying, "Why are we stopping here?" I threw the keys down to the river and said, "We're stopping to look around and just enjoy being here." This is the stuff my dad did when he raised us all. No, he couldn't afford to take us to Italy, but he would have if he could have, and he would have done it that way. Now I'm being that man, living up to his example.

What happened with me is that I got to a point where my life was too crazy in Indianapolis. I was spending money like crazy, partying three or four nights a week. I would have a limo every time I went out because I wasn't going to have something stupid happen. I had a tab running for the limo, and I just said, "Run it." We'd go out all night sometimes; I'd get a couple of hours of sleep and then head to practice or whatever. The thing is, I was living every dollar I made. Then, in the off-season, I'd be down in Florida. I was living down there and inviting teammates to come down. We'd go to the clubs, and I was running a tab. That's when my accountant called me one day and gave me some sobering news. He said, "Dude, you spent $70,000 at the nightclubs the past month and a half. You don't have the money to keep this up." The way I was living, I was going broke. As I said before, I believe you should live large when you're young. I had boats, I had cars—I had fun. But now I was getting to the crisis point.

I made the decision after Teddy Marchibroda became the coach of the Colts in 1992. I remember telling Teddy that I was making this big life move. He was happy for me, but he was a little disappointed too. He always thought guys lost a little bit of that wild side, that intensity, when they got married, so I think he was a little worried. It turned out to be no problem. What Teddy kind of misunderstood about me was that I didn't need to be single and wild to make the most of my ability. Really, I needed to be more settled and focused.

I remember one of the first times I got fined when I was in Indianapolis. It was for being late by one minute. That was it, one minute, and they docked me. All of a sudden I had a phobia about being late. I would be five minutes early to meetings just to avoid it. To this day I don't keep people waiting on me, and I don't want to wait on other people. Be on time, do it right.

I think that comes back to my old man. He was a stickler for details and doing everything right. Make sure everything is clean and right, don't settle for mediocrity. It was everything from the way he dressed to the way he ran his businesses to how we kept the house. If I see something half-assed, it drives me crazy. Don't do the job if you don't want to do it right. I was in a hotel one time, checked into my room, and when I stepped inside, it was disgusting. I called downstairs and told the manager to come up to the room. I asked him straight up, "Would you sleep in this room?" I kept telling him that the room was a reflection of him and how he did business. I was serious about that, because that's how I felt.

Again, that was my dad. If you were putting on a hubcap or sweeping the driveway, you did it right. He used to tell me when I went out to play, "You got my name on your back." I tell my kids that all the time: "You're not just representing yourself—you're representing the whole family." I had twenty-two years to learn that from my father, and now I make sure that I pass it on to my kids. This extends all the way to when I'm doing the *Man Caves* show. If it's not perfect, I'm pissed off. If someone lets me in their house, I want to do a perfect job for them. That's me, that's my work. I'm happy that my cohost, Jason Cameron, feels the exact same way. He wants perfection, and if it's not up to par, we're changing it right then and there.

With my wife, I wanted everything in our wedding to be perfect because she deserved it. Here's a woman who has been so loyal to me for my whole life. I knew she was the one, because she loved me long before I was doing anything. It's like the weekend I didn't get drafted, she stuck by me. I just realized right then—this is the person I want to be with. That's when I went home and bought the ring and came up with my plan to ask her to marry me at my father's grave.

In sports, lots of guys don't get that about women. They start making money, and they really think they have gotten that much better-looking.

Nothing makes a guy look more handsome than a fat wallet. All of a sudden, you have women hanging around you, trying to get a piece of you and what you have. Well, that's not loyalty; that's not someone who wants to have a family with you, who wants to protect you and have you protect them. That's not anything like I grew up with. Kathy knew what I was about.

The funny part is that, after we got engaged, it was like an instant party. She went crazy. She didn't expect that was going to happen in a million years. When we got home to Kenilworth, she told her family, and within fifteen minutes there were like two hundred people at my family's house. Of course, my mother was cooking macaroni, getting the sauce ready, and the other people were bringing in breads and cakes. I said to everybody there, "That's it, I'm finished. I'm done with the partying lifestyle and all this other shit. We're just going to go and pop some kids out."

Pretty soon after we got engaged, I had to go back to Indianapolis to get ready for the season. Kathy stayed back in New Jersey to plan the wedding. We never lived together before we got married because that's taboo. We're old-school, and so are both our families. So she stayed home and planned the whole wedding. She did everything. My wife is super-organized. She went and visited ten bands and said, "I like these four." I would fly home every Tuesday during the football season that year and do stuff like listen to the four bands, make a final decision, and do the deal. She made it so easy for me with all the stuff like that. We had buses of people come to the wedding. We had people from Indianapolis come out. Instead of a one-hour cocktail hour, we had a two-and-a-half-hour cocktail party. We had fifteen ice sculptures. I spent over $100,000 on my wedding.

Okay, so much for getting my financial situation under control. Just joking, honey. Truth is, that $100,000 was probably peanuts compared to what I would have spent if my life had kept going out of control the way it was. My wife wasn't just the best woman I ever met, she was the best financial decision I ever made. To this day, I'll give her a bunch of money and she'll spend a few dollars and put the rest back in the bank. I see a lot of guys in this business, their wives or even girlfriends can't spend the money fast enough—and they spend it on some of the stupidest shit you'll ever see. I can't tell you the number of guys I know from football who, when I ask them what their wives do, say, "Shop."

Anyway, our wedding was unreal. It was at the Westmount Country Club in Paterson, New Jersey, about fifteen miles from Kenilworth. It was this beautiful place, and they completely took care of us. We had four hundred people, and we had every bell and whistle. I had a mandolin player because my dad played the mandolin. After the cocktail party, we had a six-hour wedding party. It was the party of all parties. We had the people from the Manhattan Transfer, a fifteen-piece band, we rented out a hotel for a bunch of the guests—it was crazy.

I wanted to be comfortable, and I was still playing for the Colts, so I had a vest made with all Colts stuff on it. I hated pants and hated getting dressed up (still do), so I made sure the tux had shorts for after the ceremony. I wore pants for the ceremony and shorts for the reception and the party. I never sat down to eat the entire time because I was too busy. I was going from table to table thanking people, and then I was on the dance floor with my wife. The whole time, all I wanted to do was make sure there was somebody next to me with a platter of food if Kathy or I got hungry.

Basically, my wedding was about me wanting what I wanted: I wanted my wife and me to be happy every moment of the event. It was funny, I hired this cameraman to take pictures and shoot video the whole time.

Well, we were going on and on and on, and at some point the guy would have to take a break. My brothers would start getting on this guy's case, like, "Get your ass up and start taking pictures or I'll beat you." I know, charming, but that's family love.

My wife has loved me like family since before we were married, and I always felt that. Of course, she sometimes takes the whole thing a little too far, like with food. I know it doesn't exactly look like it, but I'm a finicky eater. I want to eat stuff I grew up eating, and I want it cooked the way it was cooked when I was a kid. Things have to be a certain way. When we lived in Indianapolis, I must have spent a small fortune having my mom's food, and all the cheese and meats from home, delivered. We just couldn't find a good Italian market in Indianapolis. My wife, bless her soul, is always trying to watch my weight for me. Every once in a while I bust her putting Egg Beaters in my meatballs. Trust me, I can tell the difference. Of course, my wife still looks the same as she did when we first met in high school. She's lucky that way—she still looks young and beautiful.

Actually, make that, I'm lucky that way.

13

THE TV TRANSITION

After the Super Bowl win, life was great. I met Spike Lee, which I'll get back to later in the book. I did the TV circuit, like *Late Show with David Letterman,* and I appeared on HBO's *Arli$$.* I met these millionaire dot-com guys, which led to another funny story. I opened a restaurant—all sorts of things were happening. But the biggest thing that happened was that I started to see the beginning of the end of my football career. I knew it was time to get into something else, and that final season in Baltimore gave me some more chances to transition.

Look, I could tell you that I was really sad that I knew I was getting close to the end, but that's all bullshit. Trust me, we all wish we could just play and play and play, but football is not so easy. You start to find out as you get older that it hurts a lot more, for a lot longer. The kind of stuff that used to feel better by Wednesday was starting not to feel good until the following Saturday. Your knees and all your other joints are sore for days and days and days. You don't feel good the whole week. For me, by the end, the Ravens knew not to push me out into practice every day. They took it easy on me. I maybe practiced once a week, sometimes not at all. By 2001, I sometimes couldn't practice at all for weeks.

Of course, I had been doing radio since I got to Baltimore, picking up where I left off in Indianapolis. By now, however, my show was almost like part Howard Stern and part sports. The newspapers in Baltimore referred to my show as "bawdy," which was a polite way of putting it. By the 2001 off-season, WMAR in Baltimore had bought the rights to televise my radio show. Drew Barry, the GM of the station, said: "Everybody knows that Goose is one of the hottest football properties out there. Obviously, Goose is in national demand now. He's pure entertainment." There you go.

All off-season I had people calling me, wanting to know if I was interested in this or that. The dot-com guys were around, just basically hanging out, which led to this great moment. I'm working on one of my restaurants, but I have to get to minicamp. One of the dot-com guys has a helicopter, so he gives me a ride to practice one day. It's fantastic. I show up an hour or two before practice and everybody from the Ravens is looking out there going, "What the hell is that?" Then I get out of the helicopter.

Before that season, the Ravens had agreed to do this show called *Hard Knocks,* which was recorded by NFL Films and shown on HBO. It was the first season of the show, and the NFL Films people were given almost complete access to our team throughout training camp. They didn't just do interviews with the players. They would be in our meeting rooms, on the field, in the locker room, and behind closed doors with the coaches. It was great—particularly for me. I'm not saying I was the star of the show, but I had some great moments. I got interviewed a lot, and I was in the middle of some funny moments. For instance, we had the "King Ugly" competition, which names the ugliest guy on the team. Part of the "award" was cash. Well, they caught me in one scene where I'm counting the cash. As I'm counting, I slip one of the bills under my ass. Look, it was just my entry fee; I deserved something for counting the money. The best part was, it was sly and it was quick. Hey, I learned my lessons playing cards at the Italian-American Club in Kenilworth.

Anyway, *Hard Knocks* was a huge hit; we were very entertaining. You saw a lot of Brian Billick pontificating in his own Brian way. You had funny stuff like me pulling a gag on tight end Shannon Sharpe and Sharpe demanding "restitution." It was funny stuff. Of course, some of it sucked, like us losing running back Jamal Lewis to an injury. He missed the whole season, which put a bit of a crimp in our plan to repeat. Then there was the quarterback competition between Randall Cunningham and Elvis Grbac. Cunningham was thirty-eight by then, and Grbac had a lot of attitude coming in the door. We had let Trent Dilfer go in a contract dispute and signed the other guys. Grbac said, "It's time that a quarterback comes in here and provides leadership, a go-to guy, a vertical passing game. This is a great team. I can make it better." Not exactly classy and not exactly what we needed. We just needed a quarterback to make a few plays, not be some kind of hero.

That season, we finished 10–6, made the playoffs, beat the Dolphins down in their place, but then lost to Pittsburgh in the next round. By then, I was ready to move on, so I retired from the game. It was a great ride, but my body was done. It wasn't long after that that I had all these networks calling me to see if I was interested in a TV gig. ESPN called and wanted to do fifty different shows for the same amount of money. FOX called and had just the NFL show, so I did that for a year. I flew to Los Angeles every weekend for twenty-one weeks in a row. After that, Bob Stenner was talking to me about working in the booth, and then later there was talk about putting me on the sidelines.

As all of this was going on, I still had my buddy from Indianapolis, Eddie Toner, hanging around with me. Toner was my business partner by now, although I was just trying to make sure he had a job and all because I felt a little responsible for him and everything. (Disclaimer: Toner is actually one of the smartest guys I know. He could have gone to Harvard if he had really wanted to, but he wanted to do this football thing. Go figure. He's like that character in *Good Will Hunting* who can figure out all the stuff in his head. But don't ever tell him I wrote that.)

Anyway, Toner and I were hanging out in Los Angeles while I was starting to work for FOX. I wasn't just trying to do the football thing; I was pitching show ideas and everything. Toner would roll his eyes because he didn't understand that I could do a lot of this right off the cuff. I went in and had like three offers for shows right away. Toner was looking at me, shaking his head, saying, "This isn't supposed to happen this way." I don't care how it's supposed to happen, I'm a natural at this. Hell, I came up with one concept just on all the friends I have in New Jersey, like Crazy Mike, and they loved it. I was just talking about people I grew up with, and the TV people were saying, "These are some of the craziest people we've ever heard of."

Unfortunately, a little too crazy. I called this show "Goose's Opportunity Tour." We pitched the thing to Comedy Central, and they were totally into it. The whole thing was to take all my buddies from Kenilworth and throw them in different situations, like take them to Amish country and have them mix with the Amish folks down there. Plus, we were going to have all these kinds of talent contests along the way. It was going to be great. I had Toner along with me to organize the whole thing when the camera crew came down to Kenilworth to shoot the pilot. The directors were there meeting all my buddies at the diner in town. Everything was going great. We hadn't even left the diner and one of the producers came up and told Toner, "We already have enough material for a full season." It was awesome. It was just like I thought: all my crazy friends were going to be perfect for reality TV, a total hit. We were going to make millions on this stuff. We were about to take off for Amish country. One of my friends, he really didn't get the whole Mennonite thing with the Amish, so he was walking around telling everybody, "We're going to the Amish company to see the hermaphrodite." I told everybody not to correct him, just let him talk. That was the plan, to just let these guys be themselves.

The producers thought the whole thing was hysterical. The only problem was that nobody believed it; they didn't think it was reality. They thought all my friends were like out-of-work actors trying to get started in the business. They thought, *There's no way people really act like this.* Seriously, my friends were too real for them. This would have been fantastic, better than any of that *Jersey Shore* crap. We would have been on *Leno* and *Letterman.* We would have been stars. The only problem was that all my friends started getting way ahead of themselves. They were talking about how they wanted to go on *Leno* by themselves, not with this guy or that guy. They were showing pictures of the condos and cars they wanted to buy. My friends, they're a little off the deep end.

Of course, I'm a little out there too. One day while I'm in Los Angeles back in 2003, Toner and I go into this big-and-tall store because I'm always looking for something a little different so I can look good. You never know, they might have different stuff out there in L.A. Anyway, as we're in there, this heavyset black guy and his friend come up and start talking to me. They're saying, "Goose, man, we love you on TV. You're doing a great job." The heavyset guy has a towel around his neck like he's just been working out. I'm like, who are these guys? Should I know them? I look at Toner, and he whispers to me, "Yeah, that's Ruben Brown from Pitt." Oh yeah, I know Ruben Brown. He came to Pitt like a year or two after me and then got drafted in the first round. He had just made the Pro Bowl again and was about to be a free agent. So I say, "Man, Ruben, you had a great year, and you're really looking good. Keep in shape and you're going to make a lot of money out there as a free agent. You should easily make another Pro Bowl or two." I'm working it good, but for some reason these guys are kind of going silent. Well, we get done talking, and Toner and I leave. We get outside and I'm like, "What was his problem there?" Toner is like, "That's not Ruben Brown, you moron. That was Ruben Studdard from *American Idol.* He's about to perform in the finals against Clay Aiken." I just look at Toner and say, "Oh well, fame is fleeting." I wasn't going to give Toner the satisfaction of thinking he got one over on me. What the hell did I know about *American Idol* back then? I know a lot more now.

Now, when FOX first said they wanted me to be a sideline reporter, there was no way I was going to do that. That was just dumb. About the only thing you ever learn from that is who got hurt, and anybody can do that. You can have a producer walk over to the sideline and say, "What happened?" If a player breaks his ankle, he's not coming back in the game. And unless he broke his ankle, they're not going to tell you very much, and eventually the guy might come back. Big deal. What matters to me is, if this player isn't on the field anymore, now what happens? That's what I'm there to tell you. I'm there to tell you, "Oh yeah, you bet $500 on this game, sorry, this is why you're about to lose it all." I'm talking to the regular Joe out there who is sitting at home or in a bar and wants to understand a little bit about football without getting too complicated. Ninety percent of the people watching couldn't recognize a Cover 2 defense. I know that, so I'm not going to get all technical like you hear with some guys. I'm also not going to give you all these stats and other nonsense like that. If you need all the stats from A to Z, go look it up on the Internet or go watch some other part of the show, because that ain't me.

Anyway, so FOX got the idea to put me on the sideline, but they didn't really give me much direction. I was just like this experiment, like, "Let's put Goose on the field and see what kind of shit happens." They gave me a microphone, and it had this switch. Anytime I wanted to say something, I could just hit the switch and cut in. It all evolved from there. It went from promoting other shows on FOX and stuff like that to, after a year or two down there, me saying, "Hey, I can analyze this game, let me tell you what I see." When you're down on the field, especially in one end zone or the other, you can see what's really happening—what the lines are trying to do to each other and what the quarterback really sees.

The only problem was that I was talking about stuff I was seeing and that wasn't necessarily what people were looking at on TV. That was a disaster sometimes. I'd be looking at one thing and the replay would be showing a completely different part of the play. I remember in my third year, they put a little TV screen down there for me to review the play. It was like this four-inch screen, and it just killed my eyes to look at it and try to figure out what was going on. Then they gave me some nineteen-inch screens and put them all over the field. Now I'm up to this fifty-four-inch, big-screen deal with a telestrator, two ISO cameras, and the whole deal. I could be doing the weather report down there as a side job now.

I've also gone from walking all around the stadium to staying in one end zone. Again, that's where you really get a good view of the game. The funny thing to me is, why do coaches ever want to be on the sideline? They should want to be at one end zone so they can get the best view. I get that you have to run players on and off the field, but the best view is from each end. That's what coaches study more than anything when they're watching practice tape or game tape. They want that end zone view. Now that I'm situated that way, my chemistry with Daryl "Moose" Johnston and Kenny Albert has gotten so much better.

Here's a funny aside about working with Moose. First of all, if you've ever seen the two of us, you know we're about as different as it gets. Moose is this really straightlaced, mature, proper guy from western New York who went to Syracuse. When I first got put with him, I was think-ing, how's this going to work? The funny part is that Moose played in college with Rob Burnett, who is probably my best friend from my days in Baltimore, the guy I roomed with in training camp and on the road. So I called Rob and said, "What the hell am I supposed to do with this guy?" Rob told me, "Calm down, you just have to give him a chance and you'll love him." Rob went on to say that Moose, in his core, was just like us, the kind of guy you want to be in that foxhole with when everything is breaking down. That was good enough for me to hear.

What I've learned about Moose over the years is that we really are exactly alike. As players, we were guys whose main job was to make other people look better. He was a fullback who blocked for Emmitt Smith. His job was to help make Emmitt a star. Me, my job was to make guys around me, like Ray Lewis, the stars. I was out there to destroy the blocking scheme and then let the other guys make the play. I think we've taken that mentality to our jobs now, and it's really important because of how we're situated. When you can't see the guy you're working with, it's hard to know exactly when he's going to jump in to make a point, so we have to work incredibly hard to make sure the flow is right and we're not stepping on each other all the time. Let me put it this way: It would be really easy for me to go up to the booth and for us to run a three-man crew. But if you took another three-man crew that had only worked in the booth and put one guy on the field, then it would be really hard for them to have great flow. Really, there's so much going on, way more than just us talking. Trust me, it takes a really strong working relationship to do this.

Another reason we're so good at explaining stuff is because we have a great understanding of what the other side is trying to do. What I mean is this: I played defensive line my whole career, but my whole goal was to understand what the offense was trying to do to me and to us as a group. Now I'm actually better at explaining the offense. Meanwhile, because Moose played on offense, he really has a great understanding of what the defense is trying to do and that's what he's focused on. We both have this really detailed knowledge of the other side of the ball from where we played that helps us explain what's going on pretty quick. Between what he sees from the booth and what I see from the sideline, I think we really have a good idea of what's going on in the game, and we have a lot of fun doing it.

Deep down inside, underneath his plaid ties, his pointy shoes, and his crazy overcoats, I know there's this old football player inside of Moose, a guy who really still wants to knock the living shit out of somebody out there on the field. Yeah, it's like he had a new paint job and some body work done to fix up the dents and the scrapes, but he's still that guy, just like me. He's me and I'm him underneath it all. We've worked together so long that I can tell you what he's about to say and he can tell you what I'm about to say. That's what I love about the guy.

We don't talk over people's heads. Yeah, there's some football jargon you have to say once in a while, but you have to keep that limited. Sometimes I'll be watching a game and I'll hear some guy talk about this kind of zone or that kind of blitz, and even I get confused about what he's talking about. You have to keep it to simple, basic stuff. Yeah, you can talk about a Cover 2 defense once in a while, but you better have a quick, easy way to explain it.

I know a lot of time people think announcers are way too positive, like they're kissing the players' asses. I work really hard to keep a mixture of positive and negative. If a guy runs for ninety yards, that's obviously a great play for him and he had to do something right. At the same time, I've seen some plays where I could have run for ninety yards because somebody didn't make a play. Look, we all screw up at times, and you have to talk about that. If you're a true professional athlete, you want to know what you did badly so you can correct it. If you never want to hear the bad stuff, you ain't going to last long. At the same time, the announcer can't sit there and say, this guy sucks. That's not fair.

The same thing works for me on the announcing side. I want to know when I screw up. I want to hear the criticism. Early on in my career, I did a game from the booth and I hated it. I did a good job and it was cool, but I didn't feel like I was really part of the game. Plus, they told me, if I wanted to be a booth guy, I was going to have to start at the bottom in terms of the most important games and work my way up. I wasn't doing that. Right now, millions of people are watching me on Sunday because I'm always at one of the most important games of the weekend or I'm doing something interesting.

14

SPEAKING
OF WHICH
(RANTS)

The NFL—and football in general—is in trouble. Not the business of football, or its popularity, but the game itself. I see it all the time, especially now with the concussion issue. Every time somebody gets hurt, I bet we lose a hundred kids from football because their parents look out there and say, "Uh no, no way." Even for myself, my son is thirteen years old as I'm writing this book. He was born right as my career was hitting its highest point, when we were about to win the Super Bowl. My son tells me, "I want to play football." I say to him, "You're going to own a team, you're not going to freaking play." Of course, he plays. I let him and I coach him up. He plays running back and linebacker. He has great speed, and he's learned pretty quickly about using angles.

But I see how people react to the sport now. It's like some people are scared to have their kids out there. I also know from my experience that I had plenty of "dings" when I was a player. That's what we called them when I played, those mini-concussions, I guess. Most players still call them that. To be honest, I have no idea how many concussions I had in my career. Most of the time, you just dealt with it. You took a play or two off, at worst, and then got back out there, even if you were a little dazed. I do remember I had a concussion really bad one time. I was walking around like I was floating. I was in the locker room walking around, and the trainers were looking at me like, "What the hell is the matter with you?" Think about that, I'm walking around dazed and the trainers don't even know that I have a concussion. You think that would happen in today's NFL? And I've only been out for ten years.

The league is really deep into the concussion thing, which is good. We have to pay attention to that stuff. I know I've been affected. My short-term memory is shot; I forget stuff all the time. I'll start a story and then won't remember where I'm at. People notice it all the time, especially my wife. Of course, that's the price you pay for playing. Hey, better me than my kids. But that's part of what parents are thinking about. ESPN did a story one time on guys who played in the league and how a lot of them say now, "My kid doesn't need to do this." Just like I said, that's how I feel a lot of the time about my kid playing. He can find something else to do. But he loves it, so I'm not going to take that away.

Really, though, the NFL can try to do all this stuff to stop concussions, but I think they're trying to put a Band-Aid on an amputation. The game is about hitting—hitting harder and running faster. You can make sure people try to hit the right way, but you're talking about premier athletes running at each other at full speed. You think that guys can just stop when they're at full momentum and adjust how they hit somebody? Just look at me and the Gannon hit. You think I could have suddenly held up on that play? It was impossible, and I didn't move nearly as fast as these guys. It's like I see the safeties now and how they get called for hitting a "defenseless player" or whatever you call it these days. You hear announcers talk about it in every game, but how are you supposed to play that position if you don't play at full speed? If you don't come down and hit the receiver with everything you have on those plays, it destroys the game. All of a sudden, the receiver has no problem running in the middle, and that changes everything you do on defense. Those are bread-and-butter throws for the quarterback. If he can fire it in the middle and not have to worry about his receiver getting hit, the offense is set.

That's why I think secondary is the hardest place to play these days. If you hit a guy, you get a fifteen-yard penalty, your coach is pissed, the fans are pissed, your teammates are pissed, and you're probably out of a job. If you don't hit a guy, the other team scores a touchdown, your coach is pissed, the fans are pissed, your teammates are pissed, and you're definitely getting cut. If the receivers don't fear getting the shit knocked out of them if they go in the middle of the field, it's a free-for-all for the offense.

The worst part is that half the time the refs call these penalties they get it wrong. They think they see the head leading on a hit, but really it's the shoulder and the defensive player has done it exactly right. Here's the real problem: all of this is happening in tenths of a second, so they don't get a chance to really see whether the shoulder or the head hit first. The other part of the problem is, how do you not have your head out in front of you when you tackle? Seriously, stand up right now and try it. Try just getting in position to tackle someone without your head leaning forward. Now, you don't want to lead with your head when you hit some-body. You want to see what you hit. That's good form. But this is a game of people moving at high speed. You don't get to say to the ball carrier, "Hey, do you mind if I get in proper position before I tackle you?" Seri-ously, you have to hit the guy—somehow, some way—to get the job done.

I've heard all the theories about what's going on. You have the high-speed collisions. You have the stuff on special teams. You have re-petitive hits between the linemen that they talk about, even if those guys aren't hitting at full speed. But some of the stuff you hear about for solu-tions, it's going to completely change the game. It's like when John Mad-den and Roger Goodell talk about taking the three-point stance out of the game for the offensive and defensive linemen. Are you kidding me? You do that, you might as well not even have a goal-line stand, just let the running back walk in. Better yet, make it touch football. If you make all the linemen stand around in a two-point stance (that's where neither of your hands is touching the ground when you line up), the game loses all its explosion and power. If you're a defensive end trying to pass-rush, how the hell are you supposed to get going up the field? How do you fire off the ball and make yourself a smaller target so that you can get past the offensive lineman? Look, the offensive linemen are already in a lot of two-point stances because the NFL is a passing league. We all get it, but there are still times when the offensive line has to show that it's in a run-blocking situation—if nothing else, just for show. You have to be able to at least fake it.

Plus, if you make the defensive linemen stand up, you might as well just take all the linemen off the field. Have the quarterback drop back and let him pick where he wants to throw. Seriously, the defensive guys will never touch him if you take away the three-point stance. Never, not once. Look, at a certain point you have to accept that football is a physical game. If you're going to play, you're going to have to deal with pain. You're going to have to deal with injuries. You're going to have to deal with risk. Those of us who play, we get it. We do it, and we make sure that it's as safe as possible. But you can only go so far before you completely change the game, and that's what people don't understand. That's what I mean when I say the game is in trouble. It's going to get so far removed from being football that you won't recognize it anymore.

To me, one of the things you have to do is improve the training of athletes, not change the game. I go to gyms now, and the neck machines are all gone. When I was growing up, I used to work on a neck machine all the time to strengthen my neck. I have a giant freaking neck because of that, but it helped stabilize me when I got hit, and that was important. All I ever hear now is about how the insurance companies for these gyms won't cover neck machines because people get hurt too much. Don't take away the machine—just make it so that people can't work on the machine unless they know what they're doing. That's the kind of stuff I'm talking about that has to change. I go around the league now, and hardly anybody has the big, thick necks anymore. They have little necks. That doesn't work in this sport. And one more thing: they need to start paying attention to this stuff the same way at the college and high school level.

Another thing that drives me crazy is the crowd and how much it has changed because they're charging so much money for tickets these days. When I was in Indianapolis and we went to Baltimore the first year after the city got the Ravens, it was nuts, completely crazy. People were screaming, and there were fights in the stands; it was the real Dawg Pound. Now you got people in the stands eating sushi. What the fuck is that? It's a joke. When I was a kid, my father took me to one Giants game. One, that was it. I was happy, I sat in the seat, I got a Coke, and I got a cold hot dog—and you were lucky if the hot dog didn't have a vein going down the middle of it. You sat there and you watched the game. I mean, you watched the *game.* People around you were screaming and yelling and cheering and having a good time. They were into the *game.* Now it's like no one even watches the game. I look up at the stands sometimes, and it's not everybody, but it's gotten too corporate in my opinion. The league has lost the hard-nosed, blue-collar guy who couldn't wait for Sunday. That guy right now will stay home and watch the game on television instead of going to the stadium because ticket prices are out of control. Plus, it's not his people anymore. It's not people who care about how the game is actually played. It's really a social event, and it's just not how football is supposed to be in my mind.

It's not just that there are huge chunks of seats with nobody sitting there anymore because the prices are so high, it's also all these hot chicks in really cute outfits who start complaining, "Oh, it's so loud." No shit it's loud, this is football, you dumb-ass. This is primal stuff, where people are supposed to let out their emotions and cheer for their team. The goofy thing is that it's still loud at the stadium, even though lots of people don't show up, because so many stadiums mike up the crowd and play the noise over the speakers. You're not supposed to do that, but everybody does, to distract the other team. Every team wants to have that twelfth man stuff, but it's all phony-baloney to me.

The other thing with the NFL—all the freaking rules. It's out of control. The rulebook is like a goddamn phone book now. In another ten years, you're going to have to have forty Mike Pereiras (he's the former head of officiating for the NFL who works for FOX now) at every game, just so you can keep all the rules straight. It's nuts, absolutely nuts. It's like you have to be a mad scientist to know all the rules. They even have rules about how you wear your uniform. When I came into the league, you could have your shirt untucked. Now that's a fine. You don't wear the right socks, or you don't pull them up the right way, that's a fine. You don't have your pants hugging your ass the right way, that's a fine. (Actually, I made that up, but the first two are true.) Really, what do we care about, the game or some fashion show?

They should have a rule that every time they put in a new rule they have to take three rules out. And here's the really screwed-up part: you have all these rules and you still don't know what a catch is or isn't. Like, at a certain point, you should just have some common sense about this crap. It's like when Calvin Johnson caught that pass against Chicago in the 2010 season opener, and they ruled it wasn't a catch when he used the ball to brace himself. Same thing happened this year with Cincinnati. It was freaking crazy. Anybody with an ounce of common sense knows those plays were catches. I'm not even an offensive guy, and I know that. You have to reward great athletes when they do spectacular things like that, not have some lawyer up in the booth trying to write a rule about what's a catch and what's not a catch. To me, it puts too much pressure on the officials when they call a game. Instead of calling what they see, they're thinking too much.

It's like all the review stuff they do. If you're an official, you're already freaking out because your call could get overturned, which means you're thinking too much. Half the time these guys don't know when to blow the whistle on a play. That's when guys can get hurt. Plus, if you're going to do a review, why do you limit it to two per team per game? What happens if the officials get it wrong four or five times? Look, the reason they do it that way is not because they want to get all the plays right, it's because they want to keep the game to three hours. That's what I keep trying to explain to people. It's not about what's right, it's about the product; it's about keeping everything running smoothly for the networks and making sure the networks don't get more than their allotted time. God forbid that FOX gets to sell some more ads in the extra time it would take to run the game. Trust me, the league freaks out when the game runs over three hours. It's becoming a world run by accountants and penny-pinchers instead of guys just doing the right thing. The world is being run by lawyers too. Everything has got to be a rule, or you gotta worry about being sued. You've got to say the right thing on television or apologize and pay a fine. It's ridiculous.

Now, I give the league some credit for getting the whole pay thing under a little better control. You had guys coming in making $20 million, $30 million, even $50 million (that's what Sam Bradford got) guaranteed before they ever put on a jock strap in the NFL. They hadn't even gotten on the field, and they were rich. Hey, I don't begrudge anybody making money, but you have to have guys prove themselves in this sport. This is a gladiator sport, and you can't take that out of a guy. What would I have been like if they handed me all that cash? I think I would have still busted my ass, because I have pride in what I do, but I can tell you that a lot of young guys get to this level, they get some money in their pocket, and all of a sudden they aren't playing the same way they used to. I see it all the time, and you don't realize the kind of resentment that can start in a locker room. That's why it's so bad when the rookies are making more just coming into the league than some guys have made in an eight- or ten-year career.

The other thing is the NFL Players Association—that's the union that represents the players—doing a really good job of only taking care of the younger players because those are the guys in control and they know the older guys have no power. They give the retired players a couple of pieces of cheese and figure they've taken care of those guys. It's like government. Guys get elected, and they don't go fix the problem because they're all worried about getting reelected. That's why I like Chris Christie, our governor up here in New Jersey. He came in, and right away he went after the teachers union to fix that problem. He didn't try to kiss ass; he tried to fix it. Most people don't do it that way. Instead of just doing their job, they try to worry about doing somebody else's job. In football, teams work best when all of the guys just worry about doing their little part of everything rather than trying to do too much. Just do what you're supposed to do.

To me, that's why football is the purest, most noncorrupt thing. When you go to work, everything you do is filmed. They teach you, they give you time to go and develop, and then everything you do on the field, when you're playing, is videotaped. People analyze you every day. There is so much pressure. But the whole thing is, if you're playing great, you play. If you suck, you're cut. My thing is, I don't want to see the game get hurt and lose its appeal. Football can really work to help people, really give them purpose and focus. It's a great game. Just don't mess it up.

15

LIGHTS, CAMERA, GOOSE

So how did I get my first—and so far only—movie role? As with just about everything, pretty much my big mouth was the key. Being at the Super Bowl didn't hurt either. At every Friday practice during our 2000 season, coach Brian Billick would designate a nonkicker to make an extra point, and there was usually something on the line. Nothing big, but something to make it fun. Of course, I was one of only two guys who had actually made one of these extra points all season. (The other was backup quarterback Chris Redmon.) Like I've always said, I was multitalented. If you needed a kicker or you needed a long-snapper, I was your man.

Anyway, this particular week we decided to go Hollywood with the kicker. Actually, Hollywood by way of New York with director Spike Lee getting a chance to boot one. Billick got him in for the practice and offered to make a $500 donation to Morehouse College in Georgia, Lee's alma mater. So Lee is lining up for the kick. Some of our guys are cheering a little, and some are a little in awe. Me? I'm ready to bust balls. As Lee is about ready to step up to the ball, I yell out, "I got $50 says no." Lee takes a couple of steps and hits it straight and true, but right along the ground. The ball just dribbles past the end line as we all boo. Lee takes it okay. Better than the New York Giants did during the game.

So a couple of months later, after we win the Super Bowl and I do *The Tonight Show with Jay Leno* and all this other stuff, I'm in Home Depot because my leader chain broke. I get a call, and the guy on the other end of the line goes, "Goose, what's going on, it's Spike Lee." I'm like, right, this is one of my buddies busting my balls. It's probably Eddie Toner, although he can't change that Boston accent. So I say, "Yeah, buddy, okay, later," and I hang up. Well, the phone rings again like a minute later, and this time Lee says, "No, no, Goose, it's really me, don't hang up." I'm still not buying it, and I say, "Sure, sure," but then Lee says, "No, I met you that day at the Super Bowl." I'm thinking to myself, *Oh shit, this really is Spike Lee.* I manage to stay cool and say, "Oh yeah, hey, Spike, what's up?"

So Lee tells me he's doing this movie, called *25th Hour*, that he wants me to act in. I'm like, okay, what do you want me for? He says, "You're going to be an Italian mobster." Hey, Spike, that's not exactly a stretch for me, if you know what I'm saying. I'm thinking to myself, *This is creative genius?* Sarcasm aside, Lee tells me to set up a meeting with him and my agent in New York City. So I call my agent, he arranges the whole thing, and we go meet with Lee. The only thing Lee talks about the whole time is the Super Bowl. He doesn't even mention anything about the movie until the end, when he tells me, "Oh yeah, it's a mob movie, and you're going to be a Russian mobster, not an Italian mobster." What? What do you mean a Russian mobster? I can't do a Russian accent. But whatever, I'll go do some research with some people in my neighborhood and try to figure it out. I mean, a mobster is a mobster is a mobster, right? Then, Lee tells me that he needs me to go to an acting coach. What the hell is an acting coach? He tells me about some woman who was the acting coach for Tom Cruise and his second wife, Nicole Kidman. This is getting more complicated, but I'm okay with it still.

So I go to meet with this lady. She's this little woman who's really nice. It's just me and her in this room when all of a sudden I hear all these screams coming from the next room. I mean it's really, really loud—kind of freaky—and I look at her and say, "What the hell is that? Is someone or something getting killed over there?" She says, "No, they are method acting. They are screaming to relax themselves. That's an acting class." Huh, that's an acting class? So I ask her how much she charges them to go over there and scream for an acting class. She says, "Oh, about $200 or $300 a session." I say to her, "Really? Shit, I don't want to act, I want to become an acting coach." She must have had a hundred people over there. You let them scream for a little while, make them act like a tree for a little bit, and they give you $300. Sounds like a great deal to me. She starts laughing hysterically, and I say, "Lady, you got a good scam going on over there." So we hit it off pretty good. She tells me that Lee called her and told her I was a football player, but that I was a natural for acting. Okay, cool, I appreciate that.

Well, she gets me in touch with a linguist who is going to teach me a Russian accent. I'm getting ready to take a trip to the Bahamas on this big new boat I bought, so I tell this other woman, the linguist, to give me a few tapes so I can learn the accent. I listen for a while and get the accent down a little bit. The linguist teaches me a few tricks, like how to put my tongue on the roof of my mouth so I can talk with the back of my throat.

I do all that and go back to the acting coach. She goes, "All right, get in your character, and I don't want you to come out. Whatever I tell you to do, I don't want you to come out of character." Okay, I get into character, and she starts just asking me questions like she's interrogating me. I'm like, "I'm not saying nothing to you, I don't know you." I just stay in character. She tells me to get out of character, and I say, "No, I'm not getting out, you told me to stay in. Kiss my ass, lady." So she starts laughing because I won't come out of character. Then all of a sudden she gets on the phone and she calls Spike Lee, and she goes, "Spike, you're absolutely right, he's a natural. It just comes easy, he can stay in character, he doesn't get flustered. He can do it." Lee says, "Exactly what I thought." So the next thing you know, I'm in a freaking movie. How the hell did this happen?

Now, this really starts to get wild when I show up for the reading of the script. First of all, I have no idea what this crap is all about. Lee gives me a script, and my wife reads it. She's like, "Whatever." So then I ask Lee, by the way, who's in the movie? He tells me Ed Norton, Philip Seymour Hoffman, and all these other serious actors. So I go to do the reading. It's this big room, and we sit in a circle. Lee is there, but I don't know what the hell is going on. I've never been in anything like this. He says, "All right, we're just going to read through your lines." It sounds easy until he starts talking about "call times" and this and that. I don't understand any of that, so I turn to this girl who is sitting next to me and say, "Hey, sweetheart, I don't understand any of this shit. What is this?" She goes, "Oh, that's your schedule. Is this your first time?" I say, "Yeah, yeah, my first time, I don't know anything about this stuff." So she gives me some hints and stuff like that. She's dressed kind of strange, all in black, kind of that Goth look that's big with young kids. Her hair's all messed up, and she has a rip in her stockings—just kind of weird, you know. But she's nice and helpful, so I say, "Thank you." Then I look at her again and say, "Is this your first time?" She smiles and says, "No, no, I've done a couple of things." I'm like, "All right, good, if I need any help, maybe you could help me out?" She goes, "Yeah, yeah, let me know."

So then Lee says, "I want to introduce you to our lead people. We have Philip Seymour Hoffman, we have Ed Norton, we have this guy, we have that guy, and we have Oscar-winning actress Anna Paquin." That's when the Goth girl sitting next to me stands up. Man, I'm a fucking genius. Here's somebody who won an Oscar at age eleven. Now she's like twenty years old, and I'm asking if she's ever done this before. Way to go, Goose.

I felt like a real jerk. But we read through, and then we shot the movie, and it was fun. My part was pretty small, but it was a really cool experience. I've been called for some other stuff, but they always want me to read for a part, and I don't know what the hell that means. Look, I'm a chameleon. You tell me what you want, and I'll do it. I can bullshit like the rest of them, that's all it is. Just make believe you're somebody else.

I went to this other reading at the William Morris Agency, and that just didn't work because I don't really get it in that setting. I brought my buddy Eddie Toner along, and he just screwed it up for me. Well, you know me—I found a good way to put the blame on him. Basically, I was supposed to read the script beforehand, but I couldn't focus on it. Look, I have some pretty serious attention deficit disorder. It's hard for me to sit there and just pay attention to something for more than twenty or thirty minutes. Even then, it better be something that really catches my interest. That's just how my brain works. As soon as I start to get antsy, I have to get up and move around. That's just me. Of course, I have to have people around me, and I have to entertain them, so I naturally have the acting desire in me. I just have a hard time with the preparation work.

Now, you can overcome that stuff if you're really dedicated to doing it long-term. What I found was that I'm not sure I have the patience or the desire to work at it like that. That's kind of what I discovered along the way with the bits of acting I did. Anyway, we're at William Morris and I'm doing my part. They have Eddie read the other part to set me up. As we're going along, they're telling me, "Oh, Tony, this is supposed to be this kind of emotional scene." I'm like, "Oh yeah, yeah, I got it." We keep going, and they stop me again. I start looking at Toner and saying, "It's this guy, he's throwing me off." They start us again, and I'm like, "Don't you hear that Boston accent? I can't concentrate." So we start again, but I stop and say, "I'm not able to feed off his emotion because he's not doing this right. How am I supposed to work like this?" The best part is, they start yelling at Toner, and he's trying to explain that he's never done this in his life, so how is he supposed to do this, but I don't let him get a word in edgewise. Trust me, he deserved this after all the times he has screwed with me over the years.

I did get a part that I was completely comfortable with a couple of years later. I got asked to be on *The Sopranos.* Now, we're talking about something completely up my alley. I played Frankie Cortese, a driver and bodyguard for Tony Soprano. I was in the episode "Irregular Around the Margins." I had to restrain Christopher when he came after Tony with a gun, and I even got to threaten him. I got to say that I would break him like a wishbone. Later I got to be in another scene where we were in a sit-down with a bunch of guys, including Tony, Silvio, Christopher, Johnny Sack, and Phil Leotardo, after this other character got killed. It was very cool. It was like being back in the neighborhood.

The thing about *The Sopranos* is that I probably could have done that for longer, but the whole production side was really haphazard. When I did the movie with Spike Lee, everything was really organized. We'd get in, get done, and then all Spike wanted to do was talk about sports. You didn't feel like you were just standing around doin' nothing. With *The Sopranos,* it was like this whole rigmarole just to get one scene done. Plus, some of the people in charge were really full of themselves.

It's like when the talent lady from *The Sopranos* called me to be on the show. She said they were going to put me in a couple of scenes and see where it went from there. I said, "Great, no problem, but understand that I have to go on a family vacation in August, so I'm done by then. Then I have to work in September with the football stuff." So we get to do the show.

Actors are a little different—they're the guys who wanted a lot of attention in high school. So in *The Sopranos,* you have these actors trying to be gangsters. Some of the guys, they're really like their characters. For instance, Paulie is Paulie, that's who he is. He was played by Tony Sirico, who made a career of playing gangsters in a ton of movies. Sirico knew his stuff because he was a mobster in his twenties. That was back in the 1960s and early 1970s. This guy was authentic. He had gone to prison for thirteen months for robbing an after-hours club. Another time he had pled guilty to a felony weapons possession and got twenty months for that. That guy knew what he was talking about. He even got the bug to become an actor while he was in prison. Good for him.

Being around guys like that was fun, but the rest of the group kind of annoyed me. It was like all these people thought that just because they had a hit show, all of a sudden they were more important than the rest of us. You would sit there for hours and hours just trying to do this one scene. We were in Secaucus, New Jersey, this one time for a scene, working at a sewage plant right behind the shit tank. We stood there in the weeds for like four hours, and it was so bad that I had to cover my nose and mouth a bunch of times. I thought I was going to heave. We were just standing and standing and standing. It was like grains of sand going through the hourglass, and I could see it right in front of me. My life was just wasting away waiting for these people to get their idea straight. If this was what acting was going to be like, I wasn't going to be long for this.

So after I get done doing a couple of things for them, the talent lady calls me back and says, "Okay, we have to schedule you for a few more scenes." I'm like, "I told you I'm going on vacation." She tells me that I'm going to have to change that. She has a little attitude going about it, like she just expects me to change my whole life for this show. I'm like, "Sweetheart, the Siragusas don't change their plans for anybody, not even the Sopranos. We're going on vacation, and that's it."

She can't believe I'm saying this, and again, she's coming at me with attitude like I should be thankful to be on this show. I'm thinking to myself, *The balls on this woman, unbelievable.* Look, the show was great, but that's not how I was going to live my life. If that was going to be it for my acting career, so be it.

16

MAN CAVES
AND MEGA
MACHINES

S o I get this call from my agent one day in 2006, and he tells me that
DIY Network wants me to do a show for them called *Man Caves*. With
all the ideas I have ever come up with or had pitched to me, this one was
different. I have to give the DIY folks a lot of credit. As for my role, they
needed some guy who was manly and knew a little bit about construction. Well, that's all me. Literally, shit like this just falls in my lap. I have
no idea how it happens, to tell you the truth. I just go with it.

The show became a big hit. We've done more than a hundred epi-
sodes, and it's one of those shows that guys love and even women dig.

Jason Cameron, the cohost of the show, and I get along great. We come up with ideas, he does the designs, and then I make sure it gets done. I'm riding those guys all the time, pushing them hard, but Cameron and the rest of the guys love it.

Of course, I had to give them shit right from the start. Our first episode was filmed up in Boston. The night before the shoot, I show up at the hotel where we're staying and go to the bar to get a drink. I'm sitting there, minding my own business, when Cameron comes up to introduce himself. As he's talking, I'm thinking, *Okay, let's see what this guy has.* I decide to bust his balls a little bit, so when he gets done talking, I say back to him, "Yeah, great, nice to meet you," and I go back to drinking my drink. Cameron walks back to the rest of the guys. I'm kind of laughing to myself. None of those guys want to go up to me and say anything, so I give Cameron a little credit for having some guts. Fortunately, we got over that. This is *Man Caves* after all—you have to get over that shy stuff.

It's like this all the time on our show. We have a great time doing all the caves. Cameron and I come up with the ideas for the caves based on what a guy is like, what he does for a living, or what he likes. Then I start to get on everybody's case to get the job done. Cameron is Mr. Perfectionist, which you need to have. You have to have good-quality work. But I'm the agitator, pushing everybody to get things done—which is perfect for me. The guys on the show have learned to deal with my sense of humor. It's like the locker room. You see that somebody has a little weakness, you're going to make fun of that. It's guy humor, and that's part of the show. If you can't take it, you probably don't belong on *Man Caves.*

This one time we have this new production assistant. He's a really skinny, kind of geeky-looking kid. So I start riding him a little, calling him "Urkel." Look, I've called people a lot worse. I'm talking to him, and you have to know, with me, if you don't fight back, I'm going to keep going. You have to show me something, stand your ground a little. So I keep getting on the kid as the day goes by. At one point, the kid goes off on his own for a little while. After a few minutes, Cameron is looking for him because we need his help. The guy is off crying. What the hell is that? You can't be that fragile on the set of a show called *Man Caves* and expect to last. This is not *BFF Caves* or *Girl Caves*. The kid didn't show up the next day. Whatever.

Now Cameron is always giving me trouble about how much work I do. He's always saying that every time I do something, they "cringe" because they have to go back over it. Cameron says my idea of doing things is not the same as his. Let me tell you, I put in my fair share of work. I knock stuff down or hammer in stuff. When we did the cave for Snoop Dogg, who do you think was teaching Snoop how to use a miter saw? Yeah, that was me. I know my way around the toolshed. Cameron is always giving me shit, but I'm there all the time. Of course, he's Mr. Male Model, the pretty boy. He can throw a football, though; he's tough, and most importantly, he's a hell of a contractor. That time I shot him in the hand with the nail gun—that wasn't good. I felt really bad about that one, but he handled it just like I expected—pretty much how I would have done it. He tried to tell me how he was going to need like six more surgeries and physical therapy and all this crap, trying to get me really good. I could see it on his face that he was going to be okay, so I told him where he could find some sympathy.

Really, the best part about *Man Caves* is coming up with all the ideas and doing it without spending a ton of money. You want that little bit of fantasy for guys to have at the house, but make it something that isn't crazy and completely unapproachable. Now, the Snoop Dogg one was great because what we started with was so ridiculous. He had this shed out back—the kind you'd buy at Home Depot or Lowe's. When I went inside, I looked around and said, "You gotta be kidding me." I don't think Snoop, who's six-foot-four, could even stand up straight inside this thing. All he had in there was a TV and a plastic lawn chair. He'd sit back there and either play video games or watch game tapes of his son's Pop Warner team. (Snoop coaches, which is very cool.) He had this little STEELER COUN-TRY sign over the door and a Steelers sticker on one of the walls, and that was it. This ended up being the first time we ever built a man cave from the ground up, which was a cool challenge.

So we came up with our design, and we even got Cameron throwing down a couple of Snoop lines like he's the next Eminem. He's like "fo shizzle dizzle" right with Snoop. Stick with *Man Caves,* Cameron. Now, since we had to do so much of the structure, this one was obviously a little more expensive. We also put in two fifty-inch, flat-screen TVs and this couch that ended up looking like the end of a Cadillac. The one thing that was a little different, especially considering this was on the grounds of a beautiful hillside home in California, was that Snoop didn't want any windows. He literally wanted it to be just a cave. I got it. He also told us about taking wood shop back in the day. He ended up stealing our goof glasses because he thought they were so cool. He called them the "Man Cave Shades." I like it—marketing, marketing, marketing.

Part of what was a little different about this was that we put in a pretty good surveillance system, which was important for Snoop to have with all the attention he gets. We had cameras in the front of the house, in the courtyard area where we built the cave, and inside the cave so he could check out what was going on inside the cave remotely.

The best part of the trip for me was going out to the practice for the Pop Warner team. It was awesome, teaching them how to tackle, giving them pointers on technique, and then telling them my story about never giving up. I loved it. By the time we were done, you could tell Snoop was loving it. It was serious upgrade from what he had. We had a painting of him over the Cadillac couch (built out of the tail end of a '61 Caddy by these great dudes from Jake's Chop Shop), some psychedelic lighting in the corners of the room, all of his videos and DVDs organized, his Pop Warner trophy, all of it. He was talking about being on *Lifestyles of the Rich and Famous* or *MTV Cribs,* that's how good he felt. When you do that kind of job for people, it makes you feel really good.

Occasionally, the process can get annoying. Part of the way the show works is that it's usually the wife or the girlfriend who signs their guy up for the show. That's fine, but some of the women then start to take control of it once we get there. I can tell right away if this is going to really be a man cave or if it's one of those deals where things are going to change as soon as we leave. Look, I'm not a chauvinist, but we're talking about that space in the house that's supposed to be for the man of the house. Sometimes women try to strip us of everything we have, and that's not healthy either.

So we'll get to a place and start talking to the guy, and the woman will say, "Oh, we were really thinking about this or that." As soon as I start to hear that, I head for the trailer where we relax when we take a break. When the woman starts to take over, I get really aggravated because I know it's not about what the guy really wants. It's not supposed to be the woman cave. Sometimes it will get worse. The woman will come by as we're finishing up and say, "Oh, we're going to change this." That's when I tell the guys, "Let's go, let's get done, this is not our kind of job."

It's one of those situations where the guy doesn't need a man cave, he needs Dr. Oz or some really good plastic surgeon to help him get a new set of balls.

Along the way, we make some other kinds of really great caves, like this one for an amateur winemaker. We made it look like something straight out of the Tuscany region of Italy. Now, that might sound a little feminine and not like anything I would like, but that wasn't the case at all. I completely appreciate that kind of stuff. I make my own wine, and anything about Italy is right up my alley, of course. We put some really nice touches on that one, but we kept it very manly.

We've made all sorts of amazing designs—a poker man cave, a fantasy football man cave, and one where we soundproofed a basement room so this guy could rock out and not bug his family. We've done them for Dan Patrick, Rainn Wilson, Brandon Williams, and Artie Lang. The one we did for Lang was really sweet, complete with a poker table, a humidor, and a TV that popped up out of a cabinet. The wine cave was great because we built this awesome table on our own and made it look like something you would have had to pay serious bucks for.

Now, the only problem for me with *Man Caves* is that it's a purely G-rated show, because DIY Network is G-rated. I get it, so the thing I do is just be myself and let them edit me down. I have wanted to put in a stripper pole a couple of times, but that never seems to happen. Really, I'm there for the entertainment value. I go in and bust some chops, start yelling, "What are you doing? We've got to get this done," and let Cameron do the teaching. If you go on our website at DIY, he has all sorts of videos on how to build the things that we do. He's really smart about showing people how to do things, like putting down floors, whether it's hardwood or some kind of tile. We did a hockey cave that was great because we made it an all-white floor so that it looked like the ice of a rink. You have to have those kinds of touches.

Now, another part of my job is to make sure it's all-man. Nothing foofy in a man cave. Nothing pink, nothing flowery. The point is to keep it fun. It's like football: you work hard, you put in some serious effort, but in the end you better enjoy what you're doing. The whole *Man Caves* thing is so creative and fun; it's the perfect venue for what I like to do. And we're not just doing a bunch of celebrities, where it's easy to break the bank. We're working with a lot of regular guys who have a basement or a loft that they want to turn into something special—maybe a guy who owns a deli, or a guy who is into making his own coffee blends, or a stockbroker. What we're looking for is something that guy is really into.

We do about 90 percent of the shows in the New Jersey area and travel for the special ones. Cameron is always shocked when I can get something done right away because I know so many people in Jersey. For example, we're at this one guy's house doing a man cave, and the guy has a greenhouse in his backyard. He keeps saying how he wants to get rid of the greenhouse so he can have the space. I look at him and say, "Hey, I'll give you a thousand bucks for it, and I'll have it gone in an hour." The guy is like, "Okay, it's yours." Cameron is looking at me like I'm crazy, asking how the hell I'm going to get the thing out in an hour. I'm like, "I know a guy." I make a couple calls and *boom,* I have a bunch of guys come over in a big truck and take the thing away. We do that all the time. We'll be out on a job and we need something, and I'll say, "I know a guy," and Cameron looks at me, shakes his head, and says, "Of course you do." I think he thinks I know everybody in New Jersey. Not quite, but close.

The funny thing that everybody has noticed about me is that I'm always looking for an audience. I have to be doing something to entertain people. Look, that's just me, that's why I'm a natural at stuff like this. My wife is always saying to me, "You can't be alone, you have to be around people." Hey, I'm a friendly guy, I like to entertain. This is part of how I've branded myself and why people are always calling me to do things. It's like when I did the *Mega Machines* documentaries for the Discovery Channel, I was perfect for that because I'm sort of a mega machine myself.

That kind of thing is right up my alley because it's all-man kind of stuff and I'm not afraid to try stuff like that.

The idea behind that show was to learn how they use these gigantic machines that are used for odd jobs. There was this one that allowed you to basically scoop an entire tree out of the ground and move it to another location. The machine surrounded the tree, cut a deep, circular hole in the ground, and lifted the tree out. That was awesome to see. Then there were these machines that sawed cars in half or drilled giant tunnels to create sewage lines. We're talking about seriously manly machines that guys get all geeked up about using or seeing them used. Dads and their kids love that show.

I did like thirteen of them in six days after I went out to California. I'm still surprised we didn't get renewed for another season. The most fun for me about that show was getting to use the machines. People don't know that I have a license to use heavy machinery, so I know how to use that stuff. I'd start moving around, and I was using the stuff faster than the guys who regularly operate it. We'd have a race at the end of the show, and sometimes I would win, but then they would edit it to look like I lost every time. Oh well, it was still great to work with the machines.

The thing is, I know that football helped me get where I am today, but it's just a piece of what I am and what I do with my life. I used football to get to another place in my life. I gave football everything I had, don't get me wrong. You have to be authentic when you do stuff, you can't fake it. But that's not going to be the only thing my life is about. I see a lot of other guys I played with, and when they get done, they don't know what to do. Me, I have a thousand things I'm ready to do. I'm ready to do the contractor thing. I could build a house if I wanted to and make it really sweet with all the nice touches like granite countertops. I can work with heavy machinery. I've flown planes (although I don't have my license yet), and now I have a plane. I'll jump on a zip line. I have deer heads in the basement from hunting, and I've bear-hunted. Hell, I built the basement myself down there. I make wine and grappa, and I have a collection of fine liquors. I collect guns. People don't know this, but I'm a certified scuba diver. I have four-wheelers and boats. I've been fishing a hundred miles offshore. I've caught sharks.

I have a greenhouse and a shed in the backyard. I designed and built the whole backyard area, complete with a waterfall back there. I plant tomatoes, and I'm teaching my kids how to do all this stuff. I landscaped everything around my house, even picked out the shrubs. I did the back-fill and the sprinkler system. The point is, I'm trying everything I can. I like knowing everything and doing everything. Ask my wife, I drive her freaking crazy. That's why when somebody asked me about having a "bucket list"—you know, that list of things everybody wants to do before they kick the bucket—it took me a long time to think about it. The thing I came up with first? I want to grow old enough to see all my kids get married.

GOOSE TALES WITH . . .
JASON CAMERON

Jason Cameron is the cohost of DIY's *Man Caves* with Tony Siragusa. The pair have done nine seasons of the show, designing more than one hundred special rooms for men in need of an escape. While the focus has been on Siragusa's native New Jersey, the pair have gone to all sorts of places around the country and even to Kuwait to design a special "Troop Cave" for soldiers. They have designed rooms for celebrities such as Snoop Dogg, Dan Patrick, Rainn Wilson, Michael Symon, and Duff Goldman.

"Let me preface this by saying the show wouldn't be the same without Goose. I think he really drives the energy of the show; he makes it fun, keeps it interesting, and I think fans of the show are really entertained by how he does it. That being said, he's basically a giant pain in the ass. He's like a brother to me, and we have that love-hate relationship. I love him like a brother, and I hate him like a brother.

"First off, whatever time you think you have, Goose tries to make it go faster. He is on what we call 'Goose Time,' always bitching about when something is going to be done and telling us to go faster. Not only is he the first to bitch if it's not done fast enough, but he's also the first to bitch if it doesn't look good.

"Now, since his family was in construction, he knows his way around the site. He does have skills, he just doesn't use them. Instead, he's a Tasmanian devil on the set. He yells, he screams, he eats, and then he'll take a nap. But he does liven it up. He brings a sense of humor that's so great for the show. I will also give Tony a lot of credit for this: a lot of people like him with celebrity status, like ex-athletes or whoever, they come to a show, and when it hits five o'clock, they're gone. They don't stick around. You finish everything, and then they come back in the morning. Tony stays. He'll bitch and moan about having to stay, but he'll stay. If we have to work until eight, nine, ten at night, even one in the morning, he'll be there because he knows it's important. That helps a lot with the camaraderie on the show. He's egging us on to go faster and do it better, but at the end of the day he wouldn't put his name on something unless it was top-notch. He's always riding me about how I'm Mr. Particular, but in his heart he's the exact same way.

"What Tony is in charge of is the list of stuff that doesn't go in a man cave. He lays down the law. No scented candles, no doilies—I don't even know what a doily is, but I wouldn't want it in a man cave—no throw pillows, no afghans, no fuchsia, no pink . . . whatever is on the banned list, he has the list. He's the keeper, and he makes the law.

"We've had some really funny moments along the way. During the show, we'll go on field trips, like the time we played paintball. Goose and I teamed up against the homeowner and his buddy. I just remember that, as we're playing, he's moving around and I keep thinking to myself, *Wow, he's really quick.* It's amazing how fast he is for a guy that size, but that's when you begin to understand how he made it as a great athlete. You don't think about those guys being fast, but he is.

"The most memorable man cave we did was probably the 'Troop Cave' we did in Kuwait. It was a USO tent that we renovated. That meant a lot, because you want to do whatever you can for the troops. It was this big, giant tent, and we put in a theater room, a game room, a reading room, a lounge, a computer room, and a music area. That was really cool, and they were so appreciative. Of course, it was a week in 130-degree heat, so as much as Tony wanted to do it, he bitched and moaned the whole time. I had to sleep in the same room with him that whole week and share this tiny bathroom with him. He snored like an animal.

"Then there's this memory: We were doing a man cave for Rainn Wilson in 2008. He's the actor who plays Dwight on *The Office*. His man cave was actually an office we put in his house in California. Pretty cool. Anyway, I usually show the designs for the project to the homeowners first, but Rainn has pretty serious ADD, so along with Tony, I have two guys who have ADD. Neither one of them is paying attention to anything I'm saying; they're both just clowning around. Tony has a framing [nail] gun, and he's playing around with it. I've told him a bunch of times, don't play with the framing gun, but he's doing it anyway. He's not exactly Mr. Safety, and Rainn Wilson is freaked out that Tony has the framing gun. So as I'm explaining this, I turn to say something to the two of them, and I hear the framing gun start to run. As soon as you do that, if you so much as touch the trigger, it will fire a nail. So as I'm turning to say something, I hear the framing gun go off, and then I notice, as I'm moving my hand, I can't move my thumb. I don't feel anything right away, but I look at it, and there's a nail going through the tip of my thumb, and the point of the nail is sticking out at the other side of my pinky. I've been a contractor for eighteen years and never hurt myself, but all it takes is doing a show with Tony.

"When I looked back at the tape, you can see me looking at my hand and saying, 'That's not good. No, that's not good.' Rainn is white as a ghost, completely horrified, and ready to pass out. Then there's Goose, who, without hesitation, slowly puts the framing gun down on the floor, pushes it with his foot toward Rainn, and then walks off the set like he didn't do anything. Like a little kid who just broke something. So I go to the emergency room, and of course, there's like ten people in front of me. So then I go to an urgent care facility and have it bandaged up. The doctor tells me I was lucky. The nail basically hit my thumb and bounced upward, then it caught right between the skin and bone on all my fingers before it came out at the pinky. I had a couple of small fractures, but no big deal. Of course, when I head back to the set and I see Goose sitting in a car with his agent, I'm not letting him off that easy. I'm going to mess with him.

"So I walk up to the car, and Goose rolls down the window and says, 'So, are you all right?' I start to tell him how I'm going to need two or three surgeries and I'm not sure I'm going to be able to use this hand again. Well, Goose says, 'Oh, you'll be fine.' I say to him, sarcastically, 'Thanks for the sympathy.' He looks at me and says, 'You know where you can find sympathy?' Of course, I say, 'Where?' He says, 'In the dictionary, between "shit" and "syphilis." ' Deep down, I know he cared, and I know he felt bad, but he's never going to let on about that."

17

GIVING BACK

When I played football, I was addicted. Playing was my friend. I loved it. To this day, I still have nightmares about being late to the game, being late for the plane to go to games, everything like that.

I remember when I really missed it was the second year I was out. The first year I was out I did the NFL show on FOX from Los Angeles, so I really didn't go to games. I was just watching on TV. My second year I was out I was doing the sidelines, and then we did a playoff game. The national anthem really got me going. I'm standing there, and all of a sudden the electricity of being in the environment starts to get to me. The hairs on the back of my neck are standing up, and I've got to do the opening. I'm panting, my body is going out of control, and I'm in the zone, like I'm getting ready to play again. *I've got to get out of this,* I think. *I'm not going to be able to do the opening.* But I'm ready to play, my body is taking over, because these are the moments you play for—when it's the most fun.

When I played, July was like that. In July, you're getting ready to go to training camp. You know what you're about to do: the hitting, the practice, the grueling part of it. My wife always used to say to me that she never wanted to be near me in July. It was like my whole body and mind were transformed, and I'd be really angry and mean. It's like your body is talking to your brain and saying, *You son-of-a-bitch, you bastard, you're going to take me to this place that I don't want to go.* I used to fight it a little bit. I used to be a miserable bastard. I used to be down at the beach, and my wife would be like, "Oh, get away from me. Why don't you go out?"

But I remember that playoff game, working on the sidelines and my body taking over and trying to tell my brain, *You need to be out there hitting somebody, getting ready to kick ass.* That probably went on for three or four years. That's why when people made fun of Brett Favre for quitting and then coming back all the time, I didn't. I totally understood, 100 percent. People don't understand that it's the most finite thing you'll ever do. When you stop playing football, you'll never, ever, ever put the helmet on again. You'll never, ever put shoulder pads on again. You'll never get taped again. You've been doing that all the time your whole life—practices, games—and now it just stops. That's it.

No other sport is really like that, at least that I know of. In baseball, you can always go out and throw a baseball or play a little softball, swing the bat a little. You can sort of put the baseball cap back on. In soccer, you can still go out and kick the ball around in the backyard, or go to the park and play with somebody, get a pickup game going. Same thing in basketball. You can shoot around or find some old guys who want to play at the gym. There's nothing like that in football. There's nothing else that takes you to that physical, competitive place where you spent your whole life. You never again put on the knee brace and the cleats and cross that line onto the field where you become a completely different person. You never transform into that person again. A lot of guys have a hard time with that. For a lot of guys, football is a release. You hold on to that aggression, and you can let it out when you get on the field. All of a sudden you have to learn to find some other way to get that out of you, or you're probably going to jail.

For me, I thought about it ahead of time and knew it was going to be a big change—I just didn't know how big. The thing I realize is how much of an opportunity football gave me to make the transition to the real world. I could have played another couple of years. But it's like I said before—my body just started to deteriorate. I wasn't feeling good by the end of the week like I used to. I'd be in pain all week, and then I'd see my kids and realize, *I gotta take care of these guys.* I wanted to be able to throw with my son when he got old enough. I wanted to be part of my daughters' lives. A couple more years of paychecks wasn't worth it to me. For a lot of guys, it's really not easy to make that choice. And it wasn't easy for me, trust me.

Professional athletes are the most competitive people in the world. We thrive on competition, no matter what we do. Literally, it can be a game of checkers and I want to kill you in that game. I'm going to beat you, somehow, some way. My wife knows that. We don't play checkers because I'm going to do whatever I can and I'm going to be miserable if I lose. It's hard for me to play with my kids. It can be checkers or something, and I still want to beat them. It hurts me because I have that in me.

So let me just tell you something: when you have that mentality, it can take you over. Guys go out, and all of a sudden they're in a room with cocaine on the table. One person may do a line, and then the guy who is an athlete thinks, *I'm going to do a bigger line, I'm going to beat him,* and now the whole thing gets out of control. That's why so many players and ex-players become addicted to drugs and alcohol. Everybody thinks it's because we're out of control. It ain't that. It's because we think we're completely in control of everything and we can handle it all. If you did five shots, I'm going to do seven. You want to drink a bottle of Jack Daniel's? I'm drinking two bottles of Jack Daniel's. You want to drive fifty miles per hour? I'm driving eighty.

Here's a great example: We're practicing at the stadium one day in Indianapolis. When it's time for all of us to head back to the team facility afterwards, me and this other guy get in a race to see who can get back first. I have Eddie Toner with me and another guy in the backseat of my Bronco. We're going about 120 miles per hour on the freeway and speeding on the streets. We get onto the road that leads to the team facility, and this guy is in front of me. I can't get around him because it's a two-lane road. There's this berm in front of the Colts complex and then a field that goes about seventy-five to a hundred yards before you get to the parking lot. So I just cut across the road and go over the berm. Well, it feels like we're about forty feet in the air, but we land okay, and I beat the guy to the parking lot. The guy in the backseat ends up with a big knot in his head from bumping it on the roof of the Bronco. Oh well, I had to win. That's the mentality guys have in everything they do when they're pro athletes.

These days, even though I'm paid to watch football and it's a great job, I don't love watching it. I love watching my friends compete, but I would still love to play. I'm almost jealous watching it because I know how much fun the guys are having. Football has catapulted me to other things in my life, which has made it easier to make the transition, but you can't fill that competitive hole. I'm competitive about what I do on the sidelines. I want to be really good at what I do. I'm competitive in doing television shows. I try to be creative. I'm competitive in coaching little kids. I'd really love to coach in the NFL, but I just can't put my family through that. They don't deserve it. They've sacrificed enough for me. I've seen other guys do it, like Rod Woodson, one of my former teammates with Baltimore who is in the Hall of Fame now. But I just couldn't do it to my wife. The coaching life is too hard: too many hours, too stressful. Give me the little kids to coach and I'm good. Maybe I'll do the high school thing one day, but my thing is, I want to coach the misfits, the underdogs.

That's why one of the other things I do is raise money for my foundation. It's for terminally ill kids. When I was in college, in my sophomore or junior year, we used to cut through the hospital to get to practice. You could take this elevator instead of having to climb all the way up the hill to get to the stadium. Well, that part of the hospital was the children's ward. We got to know all the nurses, and we'd bring footballs and other stuff to give to the kids. There was this one kid there, he was probably about eight or nine years old, who I became friendly with. His name was Adam. I'd spend a little time with him, maybe play catch a little and sign an autograph. To the kids in the ward, we were big-time because we were so large and tough. So I'd go through every day and see him. This went on for like six to eight months. One day I went through, and he was gone. I was hoping he got better and went home, but I asked the nurse and she said, no, he had died the night before. He had cancer. I was like nineteen years old, and I cried like a little kid. It was tough. He was the most innocent kid ever. I went back to my dorm room, and I just thought, *I can't believe this little kid I would play catch with and laugh with is all of a sudden just gone.* That day I decided that if I ever made any money, I was going to try and give back. I was going to open up a foundation and give back to kids.

The Tony Siragusa Foundation gives money to the Make-A-Wish program, the American Cancer Society, and some other things too, like Little

League. I also help out individual families, like this one woman who lost her husband and had five kids. They had no money for Christmas, and I brought them all Christmas presents. I did the same thing for one of my teammates one year. His apartment burned down just before Christmas. I actually didn't really like the guy that much, but it was him and his family, and I couldn't let him go through the holiday like that. That's what you have to do when people in your life need you.

For my foundation, all these private planes were coming in, and one of the planes crashed coming into my golf tournament. Two pilots died, and we gave money to the families of the pilots. The two guys who were in the back of the plane lived, and they came to my foundation event—they still came to the benefit. They crashed in the water, they flipped over. It was just awful what happened.

You get through stuff like that, and you do everything you can to leave a positive legacy. I know what I've been given by football, and I try to make sure that people around me know that too. It's like when I ran into Ray Lewis recently at the Pro Bowl. I was out there with the FOX crew. When I played with Ray, I never really said much to him about what I thought he should do or anything like that. It wasn't my place. We were good teammates, and I loved him, but he was his own man, whether I agreed with him or not.

Anyway, we're at the practice for the Pro Bowl, and he's sitting down on one of the water jugs. I'm just watching him, and there are a bunch of fans at this fence way down at the other end of the field who are yelling for him. They couldn't get into practice because they couldn't afford it, but they're hoping to get an autograph or two. It's a bunch of kids mostly. So he walks way over there and signs an autograph for every one of the kids. When Ray was younger, he didn't always do that. He didn't always put the time in to sign and make sure he took care of the people who cared about us, who cared about the game.

When he comes back over from signing, I say, "Hey, bro, I'm really proud of you." He says, "Goose, what are you talking about?" I say, "You see those people over there? You just made yourself a thousand more fans." He says to me, "I get it now. I used to see you do that, and I never knew why you did it, but I know why now. I get it."

I was glad he had come full circle and that maybe I had a little bit to do with that. I hope I did. I hope I was able to pass something along to Ray, and I know that he has tried to keep it going. These are the kinds of lessons that the game taught me. You get out of football what you put into it. When you couple that with the work ethic and the sense of pride that my dad taught me, you get a great combination.

Football is this proving ground for what kind of person you want to be. Do you want to be the guy who fights through the pain and comes out better on the other end? That's how I viewed it. As a result, I came out better on the other end. Way better. I still have all the qualities I learned from my parents in my little hometown in New Jersey. I was able to take those qualities, make a better life for myself and my family, and hopefully set an example for other people.

Along the way, it has always been a blast, a lifelong run of living out my dreams and laughing along the way. I've met some great people in the process. I've also met some people who challenged me to be better. Whether those people were good or bad, I appreciate what they sparked in me. It has been absolutely unreal.

ACKNOWLEDGMENTS

Writing this book about my life has been almost as much fun as living it. This project was a wild ride and always entertaining. And I have plenty of people who helped along the way.

I must thank my mother, Rosemarie Siragusa, and my brothers, Pete and Elio, for all of their assistance. My wife, Kathy, was a fantastic help and an impressive editor. Thanks also to the good folks over at David Brearley High School and all my people from Kenilworth. I also got plenty of help from Baltimore Ravens General Manager Ozzie Newsome, Ravens ace PR man Kevin Byrne, and University of Pittsburgh team doctor Fred Fu.

This project simply wouldn't have been the same without the great storytelling of Ed Toner, Ted Marchibroda, Rob Burnett, Rex Ryan, and Jason Cameron.

Additionally, I'd like to thank Yahoo! NFL reporter Jason Cole for his assistance in writing and researching the book. Additionally, the work of other reporters, such as Jamison Hemsley of ESPN (and formerly the *Baltimore Sun*) and Mike Chappelle of the *Indianapolis Star*, helped me remember the details of my career.

Don Yaeger was all I could ask for as a co-writer on this project—Don really captured my voice, my attitude, and knew which stories to tell and how to tell them the right way.

ACKNOWLEDGMENTS

On top of that, editor Sean Desmond at Random House and super-agents Jim Ornstein and Mel Berger of William Morris Endeavor were all vital to the success of this project.

In short, even when you are a larger-than-life character as large as me, it's impossible to do this kind of thing alone. Thanks to many.

INDEX